Slash Your Workers' Comp Costs

Slash Your Workers' Comp Costs

How to Cut Premiums Up to 35%—and Maintain a Productive and Safe Workplace

**Thomas Lundberg
and
Lynn Tylczak**

AMACOM
American Management Association

New York • Atlanta • Boston • Chicago • Kansas City • San Francisco • Washington, D.C.
Brussels • Mexico City • Tokyo • Toronto

Library of Congress Cataloging-in-Publication Data

Lundberg, Thomas.
    Slash your workers' comp costs : how to cut premiums up to 35%—
and maintain a productive and safe workplace / Thomas Lundberg and
Lynn Tylczak.
        p.   cm.
    Includes index.
    ISBN 0-8144-0347-6
    1. Insurance, Employers' liability—United States—Cost control.
    2. Workers' compensation—United States—Cost control.
    3. Industrial safety—United States.   4. Industrial hygiene—United
States.   I. Tylczak, Lynn.   II. Title.
    HG9964.L86   1997
    658.3'82—dc21   97-2281
                                                                     CIP

Printing number

10   9   8   7   6   5   4   3   2   1

Contents

Preface

Workers' compensation is a lot like your bladder: You need it even though you probably try to ignore it. That attitude is unfortunate, because the more time you spend developing a sound workers' compensation and job safety structure, the less you'll have to spend on compensation premiums. You'll have less accidents, less injuries, and less near misses; file less claims; see less workers' compensation fraud; and thus lessen the likelihood of an involuntary inspection by the state or federal Occupational Safety and Health Administration (OSHA). Clearly, less is more.

We wrote this book to help you develop a proactive attitude toward workers' compensation.

In Chapter 1 you'll learn about the workers' compensation and Occupational Safety and Health Act-related systems and how they provide fiscal and physical protection to both employers and employees.

In Chapter 2, you'll discover how company-based policies and programs relative to preemptive job descriptions, defensive hiring practices, vehicle usage, drug and alcohol use, written safety programs, light duty, and fraud can help you avoid problematic job applicants and keep your current employees up and running things.

Chapter 3 sets out specific steps that you as an administrator can take to reduce your workers' compensation premiums. Carefully checking employee job classifications, reviewing your company's experience modifier, monitoring claim reserves, investigating multistate (extraterritorial) coverage, and using outsiders (temporary workers) and specialists (subcontractors) can substantially reduce your workers' compensation costs.

In Chapter 4, you'll learn to leverage occupational safety and health committees, employee training, and formal and informal safety meetings. Certain training and safety programs are required—and sometimes regulated—by law; it's up to you to use them efficiently and effectively.

Chapter 5 focuses on handling on-the-job accidents and because-of-the-job medical conditions. Supervisors should know what to do before, during, and after an accident. Handling any accidents properly can decrease medical (and thus workers' compensation) costs, facilitate documentation, discourage fraud, and minimize workers' compensation complaints.

Chapter 6 is about fraud: how to deal with job applicants and current workers who would fabricate, exaggerate, or otherwise accommodate various forms of workers' compensation fraud. You'll learn how to avoid applicants who might cause problems down the road and how to keep your current employees working for, rather than against, you. Nationally, workers' compensation fraud costs business $16 billion annually; you can take steps to avoid any of these costs.

The six chapters of this book cover points, policies, procedures, and programs you can use to minimize workers' compensation costs and workplace injuries. The final section of the book provides extensive resources and checklists that catalog the specific how-tos (addresses, regulation summaries, sample forms/policies/programs, etc.).

We hope that you will read this book with highlighter in hand, marking those steps you are going to take *today* to improve your workers' compensation condition. Bottom line, this book is about attitude. You can see workers' compensation as something you do or as something done to you. Give it due consideration, and the system will do right by you.

Note to the Reader

Previous drafts of this book were written in gender-neutral language. The results were awkward, distracting, and sometimes confusing. To avoid distracting readers from the substance of our presentation, we have reverted to the traditional practice of using male pronouns and possessive adjectives when making general statements. Our aim is to present the arguments clearly to readers without offending them.

Acknowledgments

Throughout this book, we have stressed the valuable information employers can get from top-notch trade and business associations. John Kirk, with Cascade Employers Association (Salem, Oregon), is an excellent case in point. John provided us with many interesting workers' compensation comments, as well as resources and checklists. This information is contained in the Resources and Checklists section. We thank John for offering his support and sharing his expertise. He's one in a million!

Slash Your Workers' Comp Costs

1

Our Safety Systems: Workers' Compensation and the OSHA Act

The workers' compensation and Occupational Safety and Health Act systems share the same general mission: to protect American workers. Although these two systems are not formally related, they complement and support one another. OSHA focuses on accident prevention; workers' compensation stresses victim compensation. In other words, OSHA establishes and regulates the work site safety net, while workers' compensation helps those who fall through it.

WORKERS' COMPENSATION

The Workers' Compensation System

Sorry; it isn't that easy. There is no single "workers' compensation system." The systems vary substantially from state to state and sometimes from carrier to carrier. Only the basic principles stay the same. Workers' compensation is insurance—nothing more. It is complex because it directly involves four parties (compensation carrier, policyholder, state government, and employees) instead of the usual two (compensation carrier and policyholder).

The workers' compensation system can generally be described in fifty words or less: Carriers determine premiums based on general industry and company-specific information. You pay; they cover; everybody's happy—until there's an accident. Once an accident occurs, the damage is documented, verified, measured, and analyzed. The victim is compensated for medical expenses, time loss, and permanent injuries. You pay higher premiums.

All workers' compensation systems have several problematic characteristics in common. These characteristics generate opportunities for both cost savings and cost crises—for example:

▼ As the name implies, workers' compensation compensates damaged or injured workers. Unfortunately, the damage is harder to validate, document, and measure than, say, the damage related to a house fire or a fender bender. As a result, fraud is prevalent. Employers must create a proworker-antifraud environment.

▼ The financial beneficiary of a workers' compensation claim is not the employer or business that paid the premium (or the one that has to worry about future premium increases). There is little incentive for the victim to forgo or minimize a claim. Therefore, using workers' compensation insurance effectively requires a careful strategy on the part of the policyholder.

▼ Policyholders and carriers work together to minimize claims and payouts; employees may erroneously deduce that if they are injured, their employer will work against their best financial interests. This attitude can severely damage employee morale and compensation cooperation.

What You Need to Know

Just as you need workers' compensation insurance to protect your business from ruinous medical expenses, lawsuits, and governmental penalties, you need a thorough understanding of workers' compensation to protect yourself from the system. Every employer should know the following basic principles and practices of the workers' compensation system:

What Exactly Is Workers' Compensation, and What Does It Cover?

Workers' compensation is insurance coverage, purchased by the employer, that covers occupational accidents and illnesses. On-the-job injuries are defined as injuries resulting from accidents (e.g., falling from a ladder) or work-related tasks (e.g., carpal tunnel syndrome generated and exacerbated by a poorly designed work space). By law, workers' compensation coverage must usually be purchased for any business that has employees.

Appropriate (aka traditional) medical expenses for injured workers are covered by the system if the injury was the result of an on-the-job accident or work-related injury or medical condition. Appropriate medical expenses are defined differently by each state; it is important that the victim and policyholder determine exactly what medical services (chiropractic manipulation, acupuncture, psychiatric services, etc.) are covered before utilizing them.

Workers may also receive time-loss payments (partial or total reimbursements for wages lost due to a compensable injury) after a specified waiting period. *Note:* Letting employees know that wages lost to job-related injuries may not be 100 percent reimbursed can help you avoid fraudulent or exaggerated claims.

Injured workers may receive lump-sum payments for permanent injuries or illnesses. In most states, a specific injury has a set value (e.g., the loss of a finger may be "worth" $1,200). The assigned value is not affected by outside factors; a successful concert pianist would get the same $1,200 per finger that would be awarded to a piano mover. In some states, a victim may continue to get medical benefits even after receiving a lump-sum settlement. Time-loss payments, however, would be discontinued.

What Does Workers' Compensation Do for Me as an Employer?

Workers' compensation creates a large risk pool for employers, lowering individual business costs and risks. Governmental involvement ensures that businesses receive appropriate, available, and complete coverage: In most states, workers injured on the job who receive workers' compensation assistance cannot sue their employer unless the accident involved gross negligence on the employer's part. Thus, workers' comp carriers (and not business policyholders) are the ones who usually have to deal with frivolous, mundane, or extended lawsuits from disgruntled victims.

How Should Workers' Compensation Be Used?

Sparingly! High claims lead to higher premiums. Not all workers' compensation–related expenses should be forwarded to the carrier. When and where legal, paying some small workers' compensation–related items (e.g., initial screening by a physician, visit to an emergency clinic) out of pocket can help you avoid large premium increases. To some extent, your workers' compensation premiums are a function of what the carrier spends on your claims.

Who Sells Workers' Compensation Coverage?

This varies from state to state. In some states it is purchased only from the state; in others, it is sold by private carriers. Depending on the state, private carriers either sell their coverage at state-controlled rates or at market-driven prices. In virtually all states, the government plays a major legislative role in workers' compensation policies.

Where Can I Obtain Workers' Compensation Information?

State-OSHA offices (listed in Resources and Checklists Section A), workers' compensation carriers, and local trade associations are all good information sources. Local trade associations are an excellent source of area-specific qualitative and quantitative workers' compensation information. *Note:* Membership in these associations may entitle you to substantial discounts in your compensation premiums.

What Are the Responsibilities of the Compensation Carrier?

The carrier supplies workers' compensation insurance to policyholders at a price that reflects the work being done by individual employees and by the company's past safety record. The carrier processes, pays, and (if fraud is suspected) investigates claims in a timely fashion. Many carriers offer special benefits (e.g., educational seminars, safety training, databases, voluntary inspections, antifraud hot lines, early-return-to-work programs, retraining).

What Are the Responsibilities of the Policyholder?

The policyholder is required to take legal and appropriate safety measures and to supply the carrier with all relevant information (e.g., jobs performed, payroll paid, documentation of injury). Realistically, it is also the policyholder's responsibility to ensure that he gets what he pays for and that he pays only for what he gets.

How Does Workers' Compensation Mesh With the Occupational Safety and Health Act?

The OSHA Act regulations and guidelines provide workers with a preemptive safety net; workers' compensation helps workers who fall through it. Manipulating the workers' compensation system is one way a state can force businesses to comply with Act requirements. Of course, following the OSHA Act guidelines can also help a business reduce its on-the-job accidents and thus its workers' compensation premiums.

Just as there is more than one workers' compensation system, the term *OSHA* covers four separate subjects. In accordance with common usage, we will use *OSHA* to identify the system in general, *OSHA Act* to reference the statute, *fed-OSHA* to discuss the OSHA operation run by federal personnel, and *state-OSHA* to identify state-based programs.

In What Ways Are My and My Carrier's Interests the Same? In What Ways Do They Diverge?

Carriers and policyholders have the same basic goals: to prevent or minimize on-the-job accidents or injuries and to keep costs and premiums low. *Note:* Carriers indirectly prevent or minimize on-the-job accidents by rewarding employers who maintain a safe, accident-free work site. In specific cases, however, the interests of these two parties diverge greatly. For example, as an employer, it is in your best financial interest to have all workers' compensation claims resolved quickly and completely; however, in some instances, a workers' compensation carrier will not immediately close an employee's case and may impose a *claim reserve* against your account. A claim reserve is an amount levied against an account to cover additional claim expenses *that may never be paid.* Claim reserves have the same impact as claim payouts on your premiums: High claim reserves mean high premiums; unreasonably high claim reserves mean unreasonably high premiums. This subject is discussed at length in Chapter 3.

What Should I Consider When Selecting a Carrier?

Assuming that your state uses private carriers, you needn't do much research relative to pure premiums. These premium figures are often controlled by state government; market pressures do not allow significant differences even when they are legal.

Workers' compensation carriers should be evaluated based on what they offer qualitatively—for example, a constructive attitude, on-the-job assistance, immediate information and updates on workers' compensation issues, special educational or research programs, and antifraud assistance.

Your local trade association should have valuable information relative to local carriers. You can also check with organizations and lobbyists who work on behalf of businesses in your state. Consider contacting your state insurance commissioner or other appropriate state organization to determine if any particular carriers have generated an inordinate number of complaints. Employee unions also have experiences and opinions that are worth considering (and selecting a union-approved carrier makes sense, given that you will want the union's help with your antifraud program).

How Are Workers' Compensation Premiums Determined? How Flexible Are They?

Workers' compensation premiums follow a set formula. Each of your employees is assigned to a job class number that reflects the specific tasks he performs. Each job class has a pure premium based on the risk involved. The *pure premium* is the amount an employer will theoretically pay for work within this classification. For example, "secretary, in office" is a low-risk job class. The company will pay a correspondingly low premium for a secretary's coverage. Each "secretary, in office" may cost your company $0.40 (in pure premiums) for every $100.00 received in wages. *Note:* Premiums are expressed as premium per $100 (pr/100).

"Roofer—residential, one or two story" is a high-risk job class; a roofer's coverage will cost more. Each roofer may cost your company $42 (in pure premiums) for every $100 received in wages.

Note the phrase *in pure premiums.* Pure premiums are actually just a starting point. The workers' compensation carrier will evaluate your company's safety record and assign it an *experience modifier.* The experience modifier determines what percentage of the pure premium your company will pay for its coverage.

If your company has an excellent safety record, its experience modifier will be less than 1.0, and you will pay less than

100 percent of the pure premium. If it has a poor safety record, the modifier would be over 1.0 and premiums more than 100 percent of the pure premium. The experience modifier is companywide. An accident in one department increases the business's overall experience modifier, forcing it to pay more for every employee's coverage.

To figure actual premiums, multiply the total premium (pure premium per 100 times payroll) times the experience modifier. *Example:* A company has ten employees, each paid $200 a day. The pure premium on these workers is $5/$100. The total pure premium per day is $100 ($5 x 20 units of $100).

A business with an experience modifier of 1.3 will pay $130 (130 percent) of the pure premium. (This subject will be discussed at length in Chapter 3.) Clearly a business can significantly reduce its workers' compensation premiums by either using "cheaper" (but appropriate) job classes or by lowering its experience modifier.

Finally, insurance companies have the right to discount premiums. These discounts, usually based on accident frequency and company size, move a company's rate closer to the minimum pure premium.

What Kind of Paperwork Is Involved?

Companies are required to maintain verifiable records (particularly relating to job classes and payroll), file any appropriate injury-related documentation and claims, keep records mandated by the OSHA Act on their safety programs, and have certain safety programs mandated by the OSHA Act in writing (a subject discussed later in this chapter).

Keeping records really means *keeping* records. For example, an employee's medical records and analyses; exposure records and analyses; certain background data methodologies, summaries and sampling results; and material safety data sheets (MSDS) and records must be kept for up to forty years. Different states have different regulations; for local legalities, check with your compensation carrier or state-OSHA offices.

Is My Workers' Compensation Policy Good Nationwide?

A most emphatic no! Always assume that your workers' compensation policies are good only in the state for which they were initiated. It's true that some state regulations allow for *extraterritorial workers' compensation coverage* (coverage carried from one state to another), but extraterritoriality should never be assumed. *Note:* Extraterritorial statutes change regularly. Yesterday's coverage may not exist today. In some cases, a worker who crosses a state border to work even a single day is not covered. If he is injured on the job, the employer will end up paying insurance penalties, OSHA fines, all of the victim's workers' compensation-type expenses, and ensuing lawsuit settlements, among others. (Multistate coverage is discussed further in Chapter 3.)

Is Workers' Compensation Fraud a Significant Issue?

Most workers' compensation claims are legitimate, but fraud is a $16 billion a year problem. Fraud increases costs for both the employer and the workers' compensation carrier. It destroys productivity, harms morale, generates animosity, and creates a negative atmosphere for all involved.

Any sound workers' compensation policy has two goals: (1) to minimize injuries to workers (particularly injuries and claims generated by employee ignorance, laxness or negligence) and (2) to avoid fraudulent claims.

MONEY SAVERS

⬇ Check Subcontractors

It's a good idea to ask all of your on-site subcontractors to provide proof of workers' compensation coverage. Let's say a subcontractor's employee *not* covered by a workers' compensation policy is injured on the job. He could try to sue your company under its workers' compensation or general liability policies.

⬇ Communicate Continuously

A smart company invests in "communication paperwork." You can create a safer and smarter workplace by using memos, bulletin boards, newsletters, posters, and other ways to keep employees focused on safety. This is a cost-effective way to influence work site awareness.

⬇ Invest in Employee Morale

Never forget that happy workers file fewer and smaller workers' compensation claims. Investments in morale pay off in safety *and* lower workers' compensation premiums.

OSHA

OSHA, fed-OSHA, state OSHA, and the OSHA Act are as critical to workers' safety as the workers' compensation system. Understanding the Act, the system, and those who administer it can help you save time, money, and lives.

The OSHA Act

The 1970 Occupational Safety and Health Act is the federal statute that establishes and regulates safe working conditions. The OSHA acronym is also used freely to identify those governmental bodies that administer it. Fed-OSHA and state-OSHA are bureaucracies with numerous employees and an important safety mission. Using their educational resources, information base, and—yes—even their regulations can guide your business toward safe working conditions.

The OSHA Act authorizes the federal government to mandate specific safety practices and fine businesses that do not meet the specifications. Periodic updates to the original Act help keep it relevant and current. For example, the Hazardous Communication Act (HAZCOM) recently added rights to those defined by the original legislation. It specifically gives employees and subcontractors the right to know and understand the risks of their employment. Under HAZCOM, a bearded industrial electrician, for example, has a need and right to know (1) if chlorine is used on his job site, (2) the dangers of chlorine exposure, (3) how to avoid excess exposure, and (4) that his beard would interfere with an oxygen mask. A sample hazardous communications program is included as in Resources and Checklists Section F.

The OSHA Act provides extensive job-specific work regulations. Some programs—hazardous substances, personal protective equipment (PPE), lockout/tagout, hazardous task identification, hazardous communications—are considered crucial and are mandated in detail. For specific information, see the Resources and Checklists section of this book.

Note: Following OSHA regulations and guidelines is not enough. The OSHA Act's General Duty Clause also requires businesses to "provide a safe workplace." In other words, you are expected to eliminate work site hazards *even when they aren't specifically regulated.* In general, your organization will be expected to:

▼ Have a working knowledge of relevant OSHA Act standards (and, of course, follow them).

▼ Educate employees relative to their legal rights and duties under the OSHA Act.

▼ Ensure that employees perform the aforementioned duties (e.g., wear PPE when appropriate).

▼ Continually monitor job site conditions.

▼ Minimize or, if possible, remove all work hazards.

▼ Check all tools and equipment and keep them in a good state of repair.

▼ Use appropriate labels and signs.

▼ Establish and communicate emergency procedures to all staff.

▼ Investigate all on-the-job accidents.

▼ Provide medical assistance in accordance with OSHA Act mandates (e.g., if required for an applicant to hold a specific job or if the employee works with dangerous materials such as vinyl chloride).

▼ Keep appropriate employee records (regarding accidents, exposure to toxic materials, and training). As noted earlier, most medical and exposure records must be kept for forty years.

▼ Follow the OSHA Act's posting rules—for example, employers must post certain items at or near the work site, including record-keeping forms, formal notices, and the OSHA Act poster; OSHA citations must be posted for three working days or until the violation has been abated, whichever period is longer.

▼ Fix anything that generates a citation. OSHA will give a deadline for fixing a citation problem; failing to do it within that time can cost you thousands of dollars a day in fines.

▼ Provide access to employee records.
—Upon request, employees are to be given free access to their medical and exposure records (in some instances, health personnel are legally allowed to delete or summarize certain information).
—With an employee's written consent, certain designees can see their medical records (designees without written consent cannot see the records without showing an occupational health need for doing so). Designees have unrestricted access to the employee's exposure records.
—If federal or state OSHA representatives follow protocol, they can gain access to an employee's medical or exposure records.

▼ To minimize work site dangers, OSHA will also expect you to keep abreast of the following:
—Acceptable exposure limits
—New technologies
—New methodologies

—Written safety programs
—Effective personnel and performance guidelines
—Safety committees and meetings
—Communication with employees

Perhaps the best way to characterize prevailing OSHA attitudes is to paraphrase an old cliché: You can never be too rich, too thin, or too safe.

Fed-OSHA and State-OSHA

There are actually two forms of OSHA: federal (fed-OSHA) and state (state-OSHA). Although these two safety systems have the same general goals and structurally overlap, do not confuse them.

Some businesses never have to conform to federal OSHA Act standards. Instead, they are regulated by state OSHA programs, which in most cases are even *tougher* than their federal counterparts. And businesses that operate interstate have to deal with a gaggle of different governments. Basically, a state has three choices relative to occupational safety and health regulations and administration:

1. It can accept the OSHA Act regulations in full and have fed-OSHA personnel administer the statewide program.

2. It can adopt the OSHA Act's regulations but administer the program itself.

3. It can develop and administer its own OSHA type of system. All state-OSHA programs must be approved by fed-OSHA; an approved state plan preempts further federal activity within the state. Most state-approved programs are tougher versions of their federal counterparts.

Keep in mind that occupational safety and health regulations and attitudes can vary greatly from state to state, so never do business in a new state before investigating its regulatory system. What is legal in one state may not be in another.

Note: You need to investigate workers' compensation issues from state to state. For example, some states allow extraterritorial coverage (carrying current workers' compensation coverage to another state); others forbid or limit it. This subject is discussed at length in Chapter 3.

Inspections and Fines

State- and fed-OSHA use both inspections and fines to ensure compliance with regulations and the General Duty Clause. Inspections and fines are simply a means to an end—a way to encourage (and, if necessary, enforce) work site safety.

OSHA personnel have the right to inspect any facility at any time, but involuntary inspections are usually a result of employee complaints or a company's poor safety record. Listening (and responding) to employee complaints can help you avoid most involuntary inspections. Formal and informal safety meetings, bulletin boards, suggestion boxes, and telephone hot lines can all be used to solicit employee input. Your goal should be to circumvent both accidents and angry employees.

Monitoring your company's safety record to ensure it is typical for the industry is also helpful. Industry statistics should be available from trade journals and associations, industry peers, workers' compensation carriers, and unions.

Grievance or experience-based inspections tend to focus on high-risk hazards (e.g., dangerous materials or tasks). Secondary concerns include compliance issues (e.g., are all regulations being followed?), safety records (is the business keeping all of the mandated paperwork?), and safety programs (do all of the workers have appropriate levels of training?). Note that involuntary inspections are often *very thorough.* OSHA personnel will presume a problem (or problems), then pragmatically and thoroughly seek its solution. For information on how to handle an OSHA inspection (and what you can expect), see the Resources and Checklists section.

Fed-OSHA's minimum fine for a "willful serious violation" is currently $5,000, with talk of increasing it to $25,000. Some state-OSHA fines are much higher, even for nonserious violations. A few states offer good-faith reductions on nonserious offenses.

One of the best ways to avoid fines is to deal with OSHA inspectors in a positive fashion, treating them as luminaries rather than adversaries. One of the authors recently requested industry-specific state occupational safety and health rules. In addition to three inches of paper came this sound advice from the OSHA inspector: "Do what you can, dump what you can't, be practical, and call if you need help." The author has followed the inspector's advice to the letter!

Being prepared for an OSHA inspection is another good way to avoid problems.

Before an OSHA Inspection

1. Greet the compliance officer, and make him comfortable. Ask the inspector for his patience as you assemble your company's inspection procedures and prepare for the inspection.

2. Ask for and photocopy the inspector's credentials.

3. Make sure that all managers are aware that an inspection is imminent.

4. Ask the inspector the reason for the visit:
   - Imminent-danger inquiry
   - Fatality inspection
   - Complaint
   - Referral
   - General program inspection

5. Ask the inspector if the inspection is a safety or hygiene inspection.

6. Consider calling your attorney and telling him that you are about to be inspected. Explain that you have asked the inspector about the type of inspection (see number 4 above) and the kind of inspection (number 5). Also, explain that you have verified the inspector's employment and assignment to your facility and have photocopied the person's credentials. Ask the attorney if there are any other rights or issues that need to be talked about before you allow the inspection to take place.

7. If the inspection is a complaint or referral inspection, strictly confine the inspector to the area of the complaint or re-

ferral. This is extremely important, because your operation can be cited for any violation in the plain view of the inspector.

8. Assemble together the following materials so this information will be available if the inspector requests them:
- ▾ OSHA logs
- ▾ Safety Committee minutes
- ▾ Managers' responses to Safety Committee's suggestions
- ▾ Training records (in plant or on file at the central office)
- ▾ MSDS book and HAZCOM program
- ▾ Machine inspection and maintenance records (forklifts, cranes, etc.)
- ▾ Lockout/tagout program
- ▾ Other formal programs
- ▾ Current compliance with locked out/tagged out (out-of-order equipment)

Provide this information *only* if requested to do so. In these records, the inspector is looking for how well they meet the letter of the law and whether the written programs are actually being carried out as outlined.

During the Opening Conference

1. Remain calm, cordial, and professional.
2. Be prepared to discuss your safety programs:
   - ▾ Training
   - ▾ Safety meetings
   - ▾ Safety Committee meetings
   - ▾ Safety equipment available
   - ▾ Any written records

The importance of this conference cannot be overstated. This is your opportunity to explain your safety and health procedures to the inspector. Be honest and forthright. If something is not complied with, don't lie. Remember: It is very unlikely that an OSHA inspector understands your industry or even has any experience in it, so take the lead. The inspector may even be somewhat intimidated by his lack of experience and industry knowledge. Do not attempt to overpower, but use your position of knowledge and understanding to your advantage.

3. If you have any outside contractors on your site, identify every contractor on the premises (independent truckers, oxygen gas suppliers, linen suppliers, parts distributors, etc.). If this independent contractor violates any OSHA Act standard, *you* could be cited for it unless you have identified that person or company as an independent contractor; then he or it is solely responsible for any violations.

4. Be prepared to explain your accident investigation procedures. Remember that weak or vague explanations can raise a red flag to the inspector, leading to a more in-depth inspection of record keeping, accident investigations, and other areas.

During the Walk-Around Inspection

1. Before the inspection, issue any personal protective equipment to the inspector that is required (hard hat, safety glasses, etc.). Ask the inspector to follow only those procedures you expect the workforce to follow; do not, for example, tell the inspector that he is required to wear a hard hat in an area where employees do not wear them.

2. Brief the inspector about any safety guidelines or orientation as you would any other visitor.

3. Be sure a company official is present with the inspector at all times. Do not let the inspector get out of sight.

4. Each time an inspector takes a picture, you may want to take an identical picture.

5. Take detailed notes of the inspection:
   ▾ Where the inspector looks
   ▾ What the inspector measures
   ▾ To whom he talks and what is discussed

6. When an inspector points out a violation, correct it immediately, if possible. At least ensure the inspector observes your directions to workers that will correct the condition or violation.

7. If the inspector attempts to interview supervisors or management, treat this situation with extreme caution. Supervisors are considered to be agents for the company and can be held liable for safety violations. You have the right to have an attorney present during interviews with supervisors. On the other hand, statements from nonsupervisory employees do not constitute admission by the company.

8. The inspector will probably want to interview employees privately. In response to any such request, advise your employees that it is their choice and their right to choose from one of the following:

▾ To be interviewed with an employee representative
▾ To be interviewed in private, with only the inspector
▾ To be interviewed with an employer representative present
▾ To refuse to be interviewed altogether

9. Limit the inspection to the area within the scope of the inspection.

During the Closing Conference

1. It may be a good idea to have a third party involved in this conference, at which the inspector will discuss the results of the inspection and may advise you if any citations are recommended. A safety officer, for example, can discuss how the company has strived to meet the General Duty Clause.

2. You should have an opportunity to negotiate final dates for abating alleged violations. Do not get locked into a time frame you cannot realistically comply with.

3. Use this conference as an opportunity to obtain information from the inspector without giving additional information to OSHA.

4. Determine what the inspector thinks are the strengths and weaknesses of your safety program.

5. Determine precisely what areas and items the inspector plans to recommend for citations.

6. Ask what hazards were created by any violations that the inspector observed.

7. Point out the items that you have already corrected—even those that the inspector has observed. Make sure the inspector knows about every item that has been corrected during or as the result of the inspection.

8. Ask the inspector if the inspection has been completed. If not, ask him to identify what remains to be completed. Pin down the inspector on what is remaining.

9. Take complete and detailed notes.

10. As a final action, request the inspector to call you personally once the final violations have been determined. The inspector is not obligated to do so, but this request helps reinforce your company's concern for complying with the requirements. This call also provides a final opportunity to negotiate, gives you an opportunity to demonstrate good-faith efforts if you have made additional corrections since the inspection, and gives an extra few days to prepare for contesting the citation or abating the condition.

Employer Benefits From OSHA

Following OSHA's lead gives you some legal support in the event of a serious incident or injury. You can reduce your legal exposure through the use of industry precedents, "allowable risk and/or hazard" standards, specific requirements, and published materials.

Employers benefit from OSHA's insistence on safe work sites, just as employees do. But no work site is 100 percent safe. In the event of a job-related accident, you may have to defend yourself legally and perhaps publicly. You can present a case based on occupational safety and health regulations and due diligence—for example:

> "Our safety program follows industry precedents. They represent the best-known, most applicable safety practices."

> "Our safety program conforms to the OSHA Act's allowable risk and hazard standards. OSHA tacitly recognizes that our inherent dangers are at a minimum."

"Our safety program incorporates the OSHA Act's industry-specific regulations. In other words, it is neither haphazard nor casual."

"Our safety staff seek new ideas from published materials. This demonstrates our commitment to the General Duty Clause. We make improvements that are not yet mandated."

MONEY SAVERS

⬇ Identify Local Perspectives

OSHA attitudes, like regulations, can vary greatly from state to state. Ask your local business or trade associations how a particular local OSHA's personnel staff perceive its safety function. If the attitude tends to be adversarial, your safety program should stress documentation. In more cooperative areas, you can (and should) request program assistance and voluntary inspections.

⬇ Conduct Voluntary Inspections

Voluntary inspections (whether conducted by fed-OSHA, state-OSHA, workers' compensation carriers, or trade associations) are helpful:

▼ They can help you identify and correct OSHA Act violations before there is a regulatory or legal problem. *Note:* OSHA inspectors do not fine businesses for violations identified during voluntary inspections.

▼ Voluntary inspections (if conducted by fed- or state-OSHA personnel) minimize the likelihood of an involuntary inspection.

▼ Requesting voluntary inspections demonstrates that you are attempting to fulfill the OSHA Act's General Duty Clause.

▼ Utilizing OSHA resources can help you reduce research and development costs, accidents, and—as a result—workers' compensation premiums.

▼ Understanding OSHA and the way it works can help you minimize time-consuming inspections, fines, shutdowns, and other costly penalties.

⬇ Know Local Biases

OSHA inspectors in different parts of the country tend to focus on (and penalize) different violations. Knowing local biases will help you identify the mistakes you had better not make (and/or the ones you can "afford"). Your trade association(s) or compensation carrier(s) should be able to provide local lists. For example, in Oregon, the top five violations (and average fines) are:

1 Employer failed to ensure that workers were
   properly trained or supervised. $9,714.29
2 Construction employer did not instruct each
   employee in recognition or avoidance of
   unsafe conditions. $4,372.35
3 Employer of eleven or more employees did
   not have established safety committee. $530.77
4 Employer did not use all means and methods
   necessary to safely accomplish all work
   where employees were exposed to a hazard. $11,333.33
5 Employer did not have or maintain a written
   HAZCOM program. $127.50

⬇ Document Employee Knowledge

Insist that employees understand *and sign off* on company policies relative to OSHA Act regulations, employee rights, and employer programs. (See Section K of Resources and Checklists.) This paper trail is valuable in case OSHA inspectors observe a worker breaking their rules or if a worker claims that he has not been given legal treatment. Your written programs and sign-offs are a defense against expensive

OSHA fines and workers' compensation claims. For example, a charge for hearing loss lodged against one of the authors' businesses was dismissed when state-OSHA and his compensation carrier learned that his company provided and required hearing protection for all employees using power equipment, employees faced disciplinary action up to and including dismissal for failure to wear earplugs when required by the company's personal protective equipment program, and all employees were aware of and had signed off on the program.

2
Company-Based Policies

A number of internally generated policies and programs can affect your business's overall safety record and thus reduce your aggregate workers' compensation costs. This chapter focuses on corporate policies and programs that are related to workers' compensation as a function of their safety and health, liability exposure, or antifraud implications.

PREEMPTIVE JOB DESCRIPTIONS

Job Descriptions

You can save on workers' compensation by hiring carefully. Note that this does *not* in any way endorse discriminatory employment practices based on a person's gender, age, race, religion, lifestyle choices, or other category. You cannot discriminate against job applicants, but job applicants themselves can be discriminating in terms of the jobs they pursue. The more information you can supply to an applicant about a specific job, the less likely he is to pursue a physically or mentally unsuitable one.

Each job should have a written *job description*—list of duties or responsibilities—that is divided into two sections:

1. Specific tasks to be performed—for example: "A grocery stockperson maintains storeroom inventory, restocks multilevel shelves, tracks physical inventory, and manually or mechanically removes and replaces damaged or past-date products." Never end this list with "and other duties as assigned."

2. The physical requirements necessary to perform the tasks—for example: "The grocery stockperson must be capable of lifting 50 pounds from the ground to shoulder height, repetitiously extending his or her arm(s) while holding up to 2 pounds, standing for extended periods of time, bending repeatedly, spending extended periods of time in refrigeration units, and operating computer software and heavy equipment."

Good job descriptions can help you identify desirable job applicants. They can also help a job applicant avoid undesirable or problematic positions—tasks or circumstances that may be safe for others but are unhealthy, difficult, or unsuitable for the applicant. For example, after years of kneeling downhill, roofers traditionally have knee problems. If a job description indicates that the worker is required to spend a great deal of time stooping and kneeling, fewer ex-roofers will apply for it. Helping applicants avoid unsuitable jobs (and needless injuries or difficulties) will help you prevent workers' compensation claims.

Job descriptions can be defensive as well as educational. Consider what happens when a company downsizes. According to one study, 64 percent of the managers whose companies have downsized said that they are expected to increase output with a decreased staff, 48 percent of the managers surveyed said they have more direct reports, and half of these managers also said they are working longer hours and under far more stress.[1] If a company does not have written job description policies designed to minimize burnout and stress-related injuries (e.g., "Overtime and after-hours work is the exception rather than the rule," "Managers/hourly employees are expected to take their allotted break/vacation time"), it can expect stress-related claims with

---

[1]Lynn Tylczak, *Downsizing Without Disaster* (Menlo Park, Calif.: Crisp Publications, 1991). Reprinted with permission. Crisp Publications, Inc., 1200 Hamilton Court, Menlo Park, CA 94025. 800-442-7477 or 415-323-6100.

enormous workers' compensation ramifications. Consider this case:

> Francis C. Dunlavey was an insurance claims adjuster with Kemper in Iowa. A merger of his employer with another insurance company brought change: a revision of claims handling procedures, different managerial personnel and, more troublesome, an increase in workload. Also, his supervisor made unrealistic demands and constantly downgraded him with unfavorable evaluations.
>
> Dunlavey reacted to all this by putting in overtime, working from 6:30 A.M. to 6:30 P.M. plus several hours on the weekends. Eventually, Dunlavey became afflicted with major depression, and his doctors were of the opinion that stress on the job was the cause.
>
> Dunlavey's claim was allowed by the industrial commissioner and affirmed by the Iowa District Court. In January 1995, the Iowa Supreme Court agreed. It found that Dunlavey's depression was a "personal injury" under the workers' comp statute and that it arose from his work.[2]

Expectations and Site or Job Modifications

Determine the physical capabilities that are required to perform a particular job. You may have to lower these requirements, by modifying your jobs or work sites, so that you can hire the physically challenged. Each job description should include a list of possible modifications. When you write job descriptions, keep the following in mind:

▼ In accordance with the *Americans with Disabilities Act* (ADA), all physical requirements listed for a particular job must

[2]Milton Bordwin, "Overwork: The Cause of Your Next Workers' Comp Claim?" *Management Review* (March 1996). Published by American Management Association, New York. All rights reserved. Reprinted by permission of the publisher.

specifically relate to that job. If a requirement isn't necessary to the performance of a job, don't include it in the job description.

▾ In accordance with the ADA, a job or work site may have to be modified so that it can be performed or utilized by a disabled employee. For example, you could provide a mechanical lifting device or shift job responsibilities so that a particular laborer does not have to lift excessive weights or bend repeatedly.

▾ Focus not on what the employee has to do (e.g., lift 100 pounds), but on what has to be done (100 pounds must be lifted). By focusing on the end rather than the means, you should be able to creatively assist the disabled.

▾ Do not set companywide standards for physical performance (e.g., "All employees—stockpersons, cashiers, secretaries, and others—must be able to lift 100 pounds"). Inappropriate demands will encourage (and legitimize) ADA-based lawsuits.

Be aware that some site modifications have major workers' compensation ramifications. Consider, for example, the implications of a new job trend: telecommuting.

▾ It is difficult to investigate in-the-home on-the-job injuries. There are seldom witnesses, and you may not be sure exactly when or how the injury occurred. Telecommuting's inherent lack of direct physical supervision facilitates fraud.

▾ It is difficult to exert control over work site safety and conditions when the workplace is in the home. In a Mississippi case *(Ready's Shell Station and Cafe v. Ready)* a bookkeeper's "office" was her living room couch and a table. One day, her husband left his loaded gun on the couch. While removing the gun from her couch, she accidentally shot her thumb off. The injury was compensable because she had to remove the gun to use the couch.

▾ Traditional employees are not covered by workers' compensation during their job commutes (exceptions will be covered later in this chapter); however, a telecommuter who is called to the work site may be covered while on the road.

▾ Allowing clients or coworkers to meet in a telecommuter's home can create serious liability problems. For all intents and purposes, a telecommuter's job site is also your job site (and your responsibility).

▼ What would normally be considered home hazards can suddenly become work (e.g., workers' compensation compensable) hazards. In a Texas case *(Security Union Insurance Company v. McClurkin),* an on-call sales superintendent stepped on a needle in his rug. Because he was using a company-installed and -financed telephone in the home, the injury was compensable.

Numerous employers have been sued because they failed to hire a disabled job applicant or did not accommodate an injured worker's request to return to work. If you find yourself in this predicament, you must be able to prove one of the following:

- ▼ Even with reasonable accommodation, the disabled plaintiff could not perform the essential job functions.
- ▼ You could not accommodate the plaintiff by restructuring the job or redistributing the work among other employees.
- ▼ You have no vacant job that the plaintiff could perform.
- ▼ Accommodating the plaintiff would force you to change the nature of your business substantially.
- ▼ The plaintiff would have been a direct threat to himself or to others on the job site.

Warning! The bigger your company is, the more you are expected to reasonably accommodate the disabled. The courts are clogged with ADA-based lawsuits. There is one case outlined in "Employees from Hell":

A shingler for a siding chain on the East Coast fell from a scaffold owing to, according to witnesses, his own carelessness in not following prescribed safety procedures. Inasmuch as Workers' Compensation laws provide benefits to anyone injured on the job no matter who's at fault, the incapacitated employee was eligible for wages and medical payments for up to 160 months, a 13.3 year period during which the employer would have to keep him on the payroll at two-thirds of his pay, even as he stayed home. Facing a future of shelling out $28,000 a year, the employer protested the case, holding that the worker was malingering and was really physically fit. "But," the company president complains, "he'd hobble into the Industrial Accidents Board with some doctor's statement in hand, and the judge found for him every time." To add insult to back injury (the most popular Workers' Compensation complaint nationwide), when the siding company advertised an opening in management, the idled worker applied for the position. The job went to a person with executive experience. The employee sued, charging discrimination against the handicapped.[3]

MONEY SAVERS

⬇ Define Job Descriptions

As a preemptive strike against expensive lawsuits or hiring errors, you may want to add information relative to what is *not* required or expected on a given job. For example, "You are not required to work more than eight hours a day."

⬇ Specify Job Tasks

When appropriate, estimate the percentage of work time or effort an employee will spend on a particular task. This information helps applicants avoid jobs they would find too repetitive, stressful, meticulous, solitary, physically demanding, or otherwise unsuitable. Unhappy employees have more reportable accidents and file more workers' compensation claims. An ounce of prevention . . .

---

[3]Robert A. Mamis, "Employees from Hell," *Inc.* (January 1995).

DEFENSIVE HIRING PRACTICES

You cannot discriminate against job applicants based on certain facts, such as an on-the-job injury or claim that preceded major employment gaps. You can, however, make staffing decisions based on gut instincts (you should always be concerned about large employment gaps).

Past Employment

Verify all employment information: periods of employment, salary information, work performed, supervisor of record, reason for leaving the last position, and so forth. The applicant may be using erroneous information in an attempt to cover prior employment problems.

There are three compensation-oriented questions that you should ask of all applicants:

1. How many jobs have you held in the past five years?
2. How long did each of these jobs last?
3. How long were the gaps between jobs? (Do *not* ask the applicant if he has ever been hurt on the job or filed a workers' compensation claim; ask purely about gaps.)

These questions are important:

- ▼ Employment gaps are always suspect. Perhaps the applicant has a hard time finding or keeping a steady job or just doesn't like to work.
- ▼ Numerous jobs may indicate a con man who stays employed just long enough to get "injured."
- ▼ The applicant may not have enough patience to learn all of the applicable safety rules and guidelines.

The bottom line is that a high percentage of workers' compensation claims are filed within the first three months of a worker's employment. Hiring the wrong person can lead to extensive and expensive problems.

Attitude Toward Others

An applicant who complains about past colleagues or supervisors is likely to carry these negative ideas (and negative—if not
dangerous—behavior) into a new work environment. Strategic
interviewing can guide applicants into showing their true colors.

Give the applicant an opportunity to be unpleasant. What
he does with that opportunity—responding with tact, grace,
humor, frustration, sarcasm, or anger—may reflect how he will
behave in the workplace. Here are three direct methods for gen-
erating interview stress:

1. *Make unexpected comments.* You can startle an applicant
   by saying something like, "So . . . did you really shave
   today?" or "Gee, you sure remind me of my ex."
2. *Respond aggressively.* You can respond to an applicant's
   comments with, "You're kidding, right?" or "That's not
   what your last employer would say."
3. *Use interview timing.* Making an applicant cool his heels
   in an outer office for half an hour or so before an interview will significantly increase his stress level (particularly if there are no magazines lying around).

Aggression is good, as long as an applicant is aggressive
toward a job, not toward other people. There is a fine line between constructive and destructive ambition. Preemployment
attitude and personality tests can be used to help determine if
an applicant is on the right side of the line. Stress interviews are
not necessarily pleasant for applicants or employers, but many
companies use them because they can help identify problematic
applicants. Savvy applicants will recognize the stress interview
for what it is—a test—and respond accordingly.

MONEY SAVERS

⬇ Use Unusual References

If the applicant is involved in team sports, ask to use his coach
as a reference. Important behavioral clues are often found in

sports situations. For example, does the applicant have a reckless attitude? Does the applicant react violently or threaten others when involved in negative situations (game delays, unpopular calls, losing or forfeiting a game)? It is important that you avoid applicants with violent tendencies. Between 1980 and 1989, homicide was the third leading cause of occupational death in the United States, and it continues to increase. One out of every four American workers will be attacked, threatened, or harassed at work in his lifetime. The resulting physical injury and stress-related workers' compensation claims can be very expensive.

⬇ Check Out the Applicant's Car

You can learn a lot about a person by looking at his car: the inside, the outside, and bumper stickers. People with meticulously clean cars are a good bet for meticulous jobs. Applicants with insensitive bumper stickers relative to race, lifestyle preferences, gender, religion, or something else may generate stress or harassment claims. Bottom line: You can't make a silk purse out of a sow's rear.

⬇ Secure a Reference Release Form

Insist that all job applicants sign a reference release form. These forms allow a business or individual to provide an accurate appraisal of an applicant's character without fear of legal reprisal. Informing applicants that you use such a form will often stop questionable characters from pursuing employment with your company (covered in depth in Chapter 6).

⬇ Interview Defensively

Avoid costly ADA-based lawsuits through the use of defensive questions. Make sure interviewers know that they can ask about behaviors but not about disability-related problems or subjects. Here are some examples of illegal questions and their legally rephrased counterparts:

Illegal: How many days were you sick last year? Do you have AIDS? Are you taking any prescription drugs?

Legal: Can you meet the attendance requirements of this job?

Illegal: Have you ever been treated for alcohol problems? How much alcohol do you drink each week?

Legal: Do you drink alcohol?

Illegal: Have you ever been addicted to drugs? How often did you use illegal drugs in the past?

Legal: Do you use illegal drugs? Have you ever been convicted of illegal drugs use, sale, or possession?

VEHICLE USAGE

In most states, vehicular accidents are the leading cause of work-related deaths. The policies governing company cars and trucks should be at least as strict and exhaustive as those governing other dangerous tools and equipment.

Policies for Drivers

Allowing an employee to drive in a company car on company time has serious legal, financial, and workers' compensation implications. You should never allow an employee behind the wheel before determining that the employee can safely—and competently—operate the vehicle, and you must have a written policy relative to vehicular use. As a minimum the policy should:

▼ Require all applicants to submit a Department of Motor Vehicles (DMV) driving abstract. DMV reports provide the person's general driving record, including whether he has been convicted of driving under the influence, has paid any fines or tickets, or has been caught driving without insurance. Employees who operate vehicles should be required to submit a DMV driving abstract on a regular basis as well as advise the company immediately of any convictions for traffic violations.

▼ State, in writing, that employees are required to use seat belts and that using company vehicles under the influence of drugs or alcohol is strictly prohibited. If you provide car or cellular phones for employees, be sure to have a written policy covering in-transit use.

▼ When job appropriate, require applicants to prove their driving skills. Give all potential drivers a driving test. *Personally.* A driver's license (even a commercial license) does not guarantee that the applicant has the skills or expertise required for your specific job. Can the applicant use a stick shift? Park properly? Back up safely?

▼ State general policies—for example, "Drivers are expected to drive safely. The consequences of inappropriate behavior are [*list the consequences*]. Company vehicles are to be used only under specified circumstances. Drivers should inspect their vehicles before each day's work." It is a good policy for the company to reimburse training expenses relative to defensive driving courses.

▼ Provide company- or job-specific information. Define any specific driving hazards associated with your business and how to deal with them (e.g., the rules and regulations covering the transportation of chemicals or flammable materials). Provide instructions on what to do if a driver is involved in an accident or breakdown.

▼ Include guidelines for supervisors. Supervisors should ensure that employees are familiar with specific vehicles. Schedules should be devised that allow employees sufficient time to reach their destinations. Supervisors can provide delivery routes and schedules that minimize the exposure to road or traffic hazards.

Employees must read and sign off the written vehicle usage policy before receiving vehicular privileges.

Employer Liabilities

There are two ways to reduce vehicular-related liabilities:

1. *Practice regular fleet maintenance.* Employees can't use a vehicle safely unless they have a safe vehicle to use, so set up a regular program for vehicular care. Routine maintenance (oil changes, tire rotation, etc.), daily inspections (lights, brakes, etc.), and a timely vehicle replacement policy are all crucial to employee and fleet safety. Develop a separate, and more stringent, program for vehicles used in the transportation of hazardous materials.

2. *Do not allow the personal use of company vehicles unless there are overriding business reasons for doing so.* Employees can be off duty; company cars can't. Company vehicles are usually covered by a firm's insurance even when they are not being used for business purposes (e.g., during breaks, commuting). For example, your firm would be liable if an off-duty employee used a company car in a driving-under-the-influence accident (this would affect your general liability *and* compensation coverage).

MONEY SAVERS

⬇ Restrict Company Work to Company Cars

Never allow employees to perform company-related errands in their own cars after work. Your firm would be liable if the employee were involved in an accident. Inadvertently extending your compensation exposure in this way can lead to substantial, totally unanticipated, and occasionally fraudulent claims.

⬇ Document Vehicle Usage and Repairs

Keep careful vehicle repair and maintenance logs in both the vehicle and at company headquarters. Drivers should initial the log daily when they conduct regular inspections of brakes, lights, and other parts. Supervisors should check periodically to ensure that the logs are accurate and up to date.

⬇ Review Driving Records Periodically

Drivers should have their driving records reviewed and analyzed as part of their employee evaluations, and this policy should be widely publicized. People tend to focus on those items that are measured and rewarded. It's human nature.

DRUG AND ALCOHOL POLICIES

A well-designed and well-publicized drug and alcohol policy is a good example of how workers' compensation strategies can save a company time, money, and manpower.

Standards

To be successful, a drug and alcohol policy needs to be well written and widely communicated. Copies of generic-but-acceptable drug and alcohol policies are usually available from trade and business associations, workers' compensation carriers, and consultants. As a minimum, your written policy should:

1. *Treat all applicants or employees equally.* Any exceptions or discrepancies can have serious repercussions. The program may be invalidated, and "victims" (e.g., drug users who fail to obtain or maintain employment with your firm) may file lawsuits.

2. *Mandate preemployment drug and alcohol tests,* for everybody from your chairperson to your charperson.

3. *Require testing after any accident.* The presence of drugs in or on a victim can have serious compensation ramifications. Employees who contribute in any significant way to an accident should also be tested.

4. *Make provisions for random drug tests in the event of increased employee grievances, absenteeism, close calls, or violent out-*

bursts. These tests should be truly random in terms of employees and dates.

5. *Make it possible to give qualifying employees a second chance.* Qualifying employees might be defined as those with a long and successful track record, extensive training, no legal trouble, those interested in changing, or those using "soft" drugs. To avoid charges of discrimination, the qualification criteria must be applied objectively to all employees, and these employees must agree to meet special conditions (drug rehab programs, regularly scheduled testing, etc.) and sign a last-chance agreement.

Check with your state laws and your attorney before implementing a drug and alcohol policy or testing because policy parameters vary by state. Also refer to Resources and Checklists Section L, which contains a sample drug and alcohol policy.

The Business Consequences

Using a drug or alcohol test as a litmus test for new or continuing employment can lead to severe staffing and recruitment problems. In the long run, however, these problems will not be as large as those associated with managing a drug-saturated workplace.

When one of the authors chose to enforce a drug-and-alcohol-free policy in his landscaping business, he agonized over the possibilities. He had heard stories of companies losing 50 to 80 percent of their workforce when similar policies were instituted, and he did experience some staffing problems—at first. Several long-term employees chose to leave, and job applicants were harder to come by. His first help-wanted ad that referenced drug and alcohol tests drew seven responses instead of the usual fifty.

Before long, however, the entire staff was happier, customers were happier, and there were fewer on-the-job injuries and close calls. The author started attracting more—and better—job applicants. This drug-and-alcohol policy improved his overall business as much as it improved his workers' compensation position.

MONEY SAVERS

⬇ Discourage Drug Users

Don't waste time and money on drug-using job applicants. Every business should post a large sign outside the facility stating that the area is a drug-free zone and that all job applicants are drug tested. If unacceptable applicants stay away, your business is better off.

⬇ Test All Employees for Drugs

The cheapest and fastest way to communicate the seriousness of your drug and alcohol policy is to let employees know that you have tested (or are going to test) the chief executive officer. Really.

⬇ Encourage Reporting of Substance Abuse

Remind employees that most workers' compensation policies do not cover workers who are injured while under the influence of drugs or alcohol (an excellent reason for employers to test postincident). The presence of drugs or alcohol at an accident site can also slow payments to innocent victims. For these reasons, it is important that workers inform their supervisors when they think a coworker is under the influence of drugs or alcohol.

A WRITTEN SAFETY PROGRAM

Ideally, a company's written safety program is both a communication tool and an action guide. It should include general policy statements, specific equipment and task guidelines, and specific training requirements. (See Resources and Checklists Section E.)

General Policy Statements

General policy statements should address your company's overall safety and security goals. A list of broad do's and don'ts is often appropriate. General policy statements provide the skeletal framework, rather than the guts, of a good safety program. Used effectively, these statements can have a significant, positive impact on a corporate safety program.

General policy statements are those overriding safety goals and concerns that will not change over time. Think of them as your firm's Ten (or more!) Commandments of Safety—for example:

- ▼ No drugs or alcohol
- ▼ No horseplay
- ▼ No work without the proper personal protective equipment

The immortality of these goals gives them a sense of power and makes them easy to remember.

Keep general policy statements short and sweet so they are easy to communicate and use. Use no more than fifteen words per sentence. Simple words, phrases, or slogans are best. Use strong, unequitable words (*never, always, will, must, require,* etc.). Remember that general policy statements are meant to communicate and educate, not impress. You can save on workers' compensation costs by developing, implementing, maintaining, and communicating a strong safety program. Infusing this program into every element of your business will reduce accidents and lower your compensation premiums.

Specific Equipment Programs

Every organization has equipment or tools that require special safety procedures. Equipment safety programs include the specific policies, rules, guidelines, and resources necessary to mandate safe equipment operation. (See Resources and Checklists Section H for sample equipment-specific guidelines.)

Every piece of equipment should be thoroughly analyzed.

Ask specifically what a piece of equipment does. What, in a worst-case scenario, could a piece of equipment do? Think beyond the machine's overall function or capabilities to its action components. For example, the overall function of a chain saw is to cut wood. The saw's action components, however, are what will interest the safety specialist. The chain saw generates a number of safety hazards (including, but not limited to):

▼ Falling objects
▼ Electrical hazards
▼ Dangerous levels of noise
▼ Back injuries (if lifted or moved incorrectly)
▼ Sharp or moving surfaces
▼ Source of harmful dust (problems with respiration or vision)

Don't skimp on equipment analysis. Specific training and use guidelines cannot be adequately compiled before a thorough equipment analysis is conducted. Problem definition precedes problem resolution.

Specific Training Requirements

Training and training decisions are often relegated to the human resources department; ideally, they are a function of the written safety program. Adequate training begets fewer injuries and lower workers' compensation costs.

Specific equipment requires specific training. Once your company has developed the specific equipment programs, it should begin work in related training programs. Pertinent federal and state occupational safety and health regulations are a good place to begin.

Appropriate training levels should be analyzed and addressed as a function of the written safety program. Employers must balance potential injuries against the cost of training (administrative and program costs, lost productivity and opportunity costs relative to the trainer and trainee, etc.). In assessing the need and value of specific equipment training programs, it is appropriate to ask:

▼ Does our company have any prior incidents or injuries regarding the equipment in question?
▼ Does this piece of equipment (or any related tasks) have a potential for extreme injury?
▼ What level of training is necessary simply to run the equipment?
▼ Is safety naturally incorporated into this training?
▼ Is the task related to this equipment a specialized one?
▼ Does federal or state law mandate specific training relative to this equipment or task?

Corporate Culture "By the Book"

Good company handbooks—those that promote progressive policies and attitudes—can improve employee morale and thus reduce workers' compensation claims. A happy worker is a safer worker.

Functionally, a corporate handbook should be considered part of the safety program and not the other way around. Why? Research indicates that companies with positive, supportive corporate cultures have fewer employee injuries and claims.

A positive, supportive corporate culture traditionally includes these components:

▼ *Information* at any time of any kind
▼ Strong statements against employee disrespect, harassment, abuse, or discrimination
▼ Strong policies against drugs and alcohol
▼ Formal opportunities to expand, grow, and contribute (e.g., training, promotional or educational programs)
▼ Open channels of communication with superordinates, subordinates, and others
▼ Fair (if not progressive) benefits that are both used and understood by employees
▼ The professional treatment of others

Can general policies such as these make a difference? Absolutely. When they aren't functioning to improve morale—and thus reduce workers' compensation claims—they can actually reduce dangerous behaviors (or, failing that, help a business legally defend itself). For example, company handbooks should include a firm "no horseplay" policy. One workers' compensation case (*Benjamin L. Thornton, Jr.,* 46 Van Natta 2389, 1994) regarding horseplay recently worked its way through the Oregon courts. It seems the claimant was injured in a water fight. Horseplay of this type had been going on at the job site for years. Even supervisors participated. Apparently the general manager wanted the horseplay to stop, but employees had not been notified of the prohibition of horseplay and were not warned of any related sanctions. The Oregon courts and the Workers' Compensation Board found that an employee injured while engaging in horseplay has a legitimate workers' compensation claim *unless* the employer has an enforced policy that forbids it.

MONEY SAVERS

↓ Check Others' Perspectives (Method 1)

Conduct a "snickers test" on all written safety programs. Ask a well-informed subordinate to read all of your safety policies and programs aloud. If he can't do that without snickering ("No drugs! Ha ha! What planet are you guys from?"), fidgeting, or frowning, you've got a problem—a serious problem.

↓ Check Others' Perspectives (Method 2)

Conduct a *"Wall Street Journal"* test on all written safety materials. Ask yourself how the material would play if it were read to the general public, particularly if the reading took place after a highly publicized on-the-job accident or fatality. Would you look as if you had done your job, or had only done the minimum?

MORALE-BUILDING POLICIES

A positive attitude and approach toward employees and their challenges can help you minimize workers' compensation costs and maximize employee morale. Communicating this approach to employees will fulfill the potential of these policies.

Return-to-Work Policy

You should have a written policy stating that, as a condition of employment, workers must be willing to accept a medically appropriate light duty assignment if they are injured while on the job. Light-duty policies are important: They get injured workers back to work and move unnecessary expenses off your workers' compensation account. (They are discussed in depth in Chapter 5.)

Light-duty policies make your company a less appealing target for workers' compensation fraud. Most frauds want to take the money and run. Faking a disability eight hours a day is no picnic. A policy that helps injured employees remain gainfully employed will repel those applicants who do not want to be gainfully employed in the first place.

In some cases (usually those that do not involve an employees' union), it is permissible to pay an injured worker wages commensurate with the light duty performed (less than he was making on his regular job). Workers are less likely to fraudulently extend their claims when it harms their finances.

Antifraud Policy

Communicate to all job applicants that you will not tolerate fraudulent workers' compensation claims. State unequivocally that you and your carrier will investigate all questionable claims, reward informants, and prosecute frauds.

It is up to you to create an antifraud environment. One way to do that is to help employees develop a zero tolerance for cheats by explaining how they might be hurt by someone else's fraud—for example:

▼ Point out that workers' compensation fraud will reduce company profits and thus what workers will earn as the result of a profit-sharing plan.

▾ Stress fairness. Remind employees of the hours they put in each week for their paychecks. Is it fair to them when, as the result of a fraudulent workers' compensation claim, a former coworker gets a similar income for doing nothing?

▾ Remind employees that they are the ones who have to make up the lost productivity when an employee is inappropriately away from work.

Be careful to differentiate between true need and basic greed. Nobody—managers, supervisors, employees, or carriers—should begrudge injured employees a legitimate claim. Injuries can happen to anyone, and workers' compensation coverage is there for everyone. However, it is everybody's job—and in everybody's self-interest—to be a part of the antifraud squad. (Fraud is discussed in depth in Chapter 6.)

MONEY SAVERS

⬇ Educate Employees About Benefits

Continually communicate all beneficial company programs and policies to employees. An unknown or unused benefit is no benefit at all, to employees or to morale. Never assume that your workers are mind (or corporate handbook) readers. Actively inform them. For example, according to Towers Perrin, over 78 percent of U.S. employers have early-return-to-work programs, yet a concurrent study by a national managed care company found that only 33 percent of American workers were aware of this benefit.

⬇ Promote Positive Programs

Use your early-return-to-work and light-duty policy to demonstrate to employees that you will not callously abandon those who are injured. These programs improve employee morale, reduce work site stress, and encourage workers to report minor injuries or problems—all of which help reduce workers' compensation claims.

3

Using the System
to Save

Although every chapter in this book contains Money Savers—ideas that will lower your workers' compensation costs—this chapter is special.

Most suggestions for reducing accidents and compensation premiums require significant changes in basic policies, procedures, and practices. In essence, they affect a firm's identity, its organizational culture, the way it does "internal business." The ideas in this chapter mostly affect peripheral paperwork. You can implement some of them without your workforce's even noticing. Because these changes are quick, easy, and inexpensive to adopt, you can expect maximum payback from minimal efforts.

JOB CLASSIFICATIONS

Job classifications are a major component of the workers' compensation system. A worker's job classification directly affects the cost of his coverage. Using the cheapest appropriate job class to categorize a worker or task can save your organization thousands of dollars every year.

Job Classes by Type

Every job has its own classification number. Jobs are grouped according to tasks performed, materials and machinery used, where the work is performed, the risks involved, training required, etc. Job names alone are misleading; there could be a dozen classification numbers under a general title or subject.

Most states use the job classification system developed by the National Council on Compensation Insurance (NCCI), although a few states have created their own categories and systems. Different classification systems can create significant problems for multistate businesses.

Job classifications are often complicated and convoluted. Take this job class description excerpted from NCCI's *Scopes Manual:*

Class 5183 applies to your employees involved in direct labor, supervision and driving who are engaged in plumbing not included within another classification. This class is applicable to gas, steam, hot water or other types of pipe fitting and includes the installation and repair of piping, fixtures, appliances, and appurtenances in connection with water supplies, drainage systems, etc. No limitations have been established as to the size of the pipe being repaired or installed. This class applies to excavation or laying of service lines only between the mainline and the building if other plumbing work is also performed by you on the same contract. Sewer cleaning between the mainline and the building is included within this class if performed with the use of portable equipment. This class also applies to the installation of underground lawn sprinkler systems. Irrigation and drainage systems construction is to be classed as 6229. Class 5183 includes work performed at your shop as well as at your customer's location. Class 5183 applies to the work inside of buildings for the installation or repair of pneumatic carrier systems. Class 5183 also applies to the repair or maintenance of your equipment, structures, buildings and vehicles used for this work. Specialty contracts only for plumbing work on commercial or residential air conditioning, heating and refrigeration systems are also subject to Class 5183. The installation of automatic sprinkler systems of the indoor type used for fire prevention purposes is properly classed as 5188— Automatic Sprinkler Installation. Installation, service, or repair of commercial or residential air conditioning, heating, and refrigeration systems is classed as 5537— Air Conditioning/Heating/Refrigeration–Installation/ Service/Repair.[1]

Warning! Misclassifying employees can have serious repercussions for a business, particularly when the error favors the employer—that is, the employee is included in a lower-cost category. Your compensation coverage could be cancelled, an injured worker's claim could be denied, or your firm could be audited (and perhaps even charged with fraud). When in doubt, query your carrier. In writing.

Premiums as a Function of Job Classification

Some employees cost less to insure than others because of their job classification. Compensation carriers assign every job classification a *pure premium*. This premium is expressed as a function of payroll. If the pure premium for Job Class 400 is $15 pr/100, you pay $15 in workers' compensation premiums for every $100 you pay in wages to a Job Class 400 employee. In other words, the amount you pay to cover an employee is a direct function of that person's job classification and his wages.

Classifying employees under the cheapest appropriate job category can save your company thousands of dollars. In one state, workers classified as landscape gardening cost employers

---

[1]National Council on Compensation Insurance, *Scopes Manual* (1995). Copyright National Council on Compensation Insurance, Inc. All rights reserved. Reprinted with permission.

$10.38 for every $100.00 in payroll. For lawn maintenance the premium is only $5.68. Carefully keeping these tasks or jobs separate would save an employer 45 percent on compensation premiums.

Here's another example: The pure premium for the job classification "carpentry-nonresidential" is $15.65 per $100.00. For "carpentry–finish work only" the premium is $7.04. Moving finish work carpenters into the appropriate job classification could save a business over 60 percent on its premiums—a hefty return for a simple, one-time change.

Note: Pure premiums are figured on an industry-wide basis. They are adjusted by a multiplier (Experience Modifier or ER Mod), which reflects each business's actual safety record.

Cutting Classification Costs

Separating payroll by workers or the jobs they do can generate significant savings. There is, however, an additional administrative burden on employees and the payroll department. Jobs must be analyzed to determine which job class or payroll reporting technique will generate the greatest corporate savings.

There are three reporting options:

1. *Separating payroll information by individual employees.* Each worker can be assigned a single job classification code and a limited range of tasks (e.g., those allowed by his code). This is the simplest—but not necessarily the most reasonable— classification approach. Record keeping is easy, but you lose a lot of productive flexibility. Most managers prefer to assign workers and tasks based on current corporate needs, not workers' compensation limitations.

2. *Separating payroll information by the day.* Every day each worker is assigned a job classification number that reflects what he did (or will do) for the majority of that day. You use the broadest classification that would cover all of the day's tasks. If Kris spends 4.5 hours roofing and 3.5 hours preparing a written estimate, Kris's employer would pay the roofer's rate for his workers' compensation coverage. The roofer's rate would legally cover Kris for the estimating work.

This approach has its own drawbacks. The broadest class will also be the most expensive. If Kris spends 4.5 hours roofing (pure premium $24.79/$100.00) and 3.5 hours preparing a bid ($0.69/$100.00), his daily workers' compensation premium would be unnecessarily high.

3. *Separating payroll information by the hour.* Each worker keeps hourly records of work performed. The payroll department then assigns each hour's wages to the appropriate job classification. In Kris's case, his employer would pay for $24.79/$100.00 on 4.5 hours of roofing work and $0.69/$100.00 for 3.5 hours of estimating. This reporting approach obviously cuts workers' compensation premium costs, but it can be a bookkeeping and a supervisory nightmare. Careful and extensive payroll records must be kept, and employees must be reminded to keep an accurate written log of their efforts.

Whatever approach you decide to take, verifiable and complete job and payroll records are a must. Note that job names, classification numbers, and short classification descriptions are included on the time card to facilitate its use. This is important if you have employees who utilize multiple job classifications.

MONEY SAVERS

⬇ Focus on the Bottom Line

Always think in terms of aggregate savings. Saving $1.00 in premiums is no deal if it costs you $1.50 to track the different payroll categories. Determine the cost difference between each employee's job classifications. If the differences are small (or the administrative or supervisory burden is large), don't divide wages between job classes. Pay for the more expensive job classification.

⬇ Schedule Strategically

Schedule or encourage employees to take advantage of your classification tracking system. For example, employees who are limited to a single expensive job class should not regularly perform low-risk, low-premium work. Jobs can also be designed to fit certain job classifications and minimize workers' compensation premiums.

⬇ Consider Trade-Offs

Offering greater benefits in lieu of higher salaries can help you save on your workers' compensation. Ask employees what (tax-free) benefits they would like to receive instead of an across-the-board wage increase. For example, instead of paying an employee $1,000 in wages and deducting $250 for medical insurance, your company can pay $750 in wages and $250 in medical benefits. Your company pays compensation premiums on $750 instead of $1,000 and the worker enjoys more after-tax income.

⬇ Stay Current

Keep file copies of all applicable job classifications. You should periodically compare jobs to job class descriptions to ensure that they still match. Often jobs expand over time to include tasks not covered by their original job classification.

⬇ Identify Trouble Spots

Give your workers' compensation paperwork a thorough inspection, and identify those documentation or recording errors that are likely to recur. Once that is done, you can develop a simple review and inspection routine that allows you to delegate follow-up responsibilities to a secretary or clerk.

⬇ Check for Profitability

Analyzing task-specific time cards can help you verify the profitability of individual tasks or services. If a task is inherently unprofitable, don't try to make it up on volume.

EXPERIENCE MODIFIERS

Experience modifiers (often referred to as *ER Mods*) are a primary determinant in setting workers' compensation premiums. They are different from job classes and pure premiums in that they are company specific. Strategic management practices can lower your company's experience modifier and, thus, its workers' compensation costs.

The Experience Modifier: A Definition

Few companies actually pay pure premium rates for their workers' compensation. Pure premiums are weighted by an organization's experience modifier, which reflects its safety track record. Pure premium times experience modification equals your company's *true premium.* You may pay more or less than the pure premium.

Experience modifiers are always expressed as a percentage of the pure premium, and they are companywide. If your firm's ER Mod is 1.2, your workers' compensation cost on every employee is 120 percent of the pure premium. If your ER Mod is 0.8, you will pay 80 percent.

Because of experience modifiers, a single compensation claim can have serious financial repercussions. Consider a company with a good safety record and an ER Mod of 0.8. One of its employees takes a fall, and, as a result, the firm's ER Mod increases to 1.2. The firm's monthly pure premium for all employees is $1,000. Before the employee's fall, its actual monthly premium was $800; now it pays $1,200.

Note: Even accident-free companies are assigned a ballast factor to cover a potential injury. For example, the experience modification for the author's firm accident free, cannot drop below 0.76.

Lowering Your Experience Modifier

Your experience modifier is based largely on what your workers' compensation carrier has paid out on your behalf. If your carrier has had to pay significant medical and disability claims, your ER Mod is going to be high. It follows that you should design programs that minimize medical and disability costs.

A thorough program audit can help you identify areas where medical expenses could be trimmed.

How to Reduce Medical Costs

1. Perform simple first aid (treating cuts or poison oak) in-house.
2. Have hurt employees go to the emergency room or doctor only when necessary.
3. Pay small claims out of pocket (if legal in your state).
4. Train employees to recognize serious safety problems.
5. Insist on proper use of personal protective equipment.
6. Conduct appropriate preemployment tests (dexterity, strength, vision, drug).
7. Invest in ergonomics (split keyboards, adjustable chairs, etc.).
8. Analyze and redesign jobs to minimize any problem areas.
9. Use subcontractors or temporary help when appropriate.

Experience modifiers aside, no company wants to harm its injured workers by withholding or reducing legitimate disability payouts. Note the word *legitimate*. If you have reason to believe that a worker is pursuing a false claim (or exaggerating or extending a legitimate one) you have to take action. Fraud is not to be tolerated.

Making fraud unappetizing is one way to reduce (if not eliminate) its potential impact on your firm's experience modifier.

True story: Frank loved to fish. Three years in a row, Frank "hurt his back" just before fishing season (he traditionally recovered a few days after opening weekend). Because his injury typically lasted more than three days, it was legally classified as a time-loss injury, a temporary disability. Frank and his "fisherman's back" cost his employer a great deal of money. The fourth year when Frank hurt his back, the company's personnel director set up a cot in a busy reception area. Frank was told to stay on the cot and take a physical inventory of pencils ("Make sure there really are 500 per box"). Frank's recovery was . . . miraculous. Frank never had another back problem (and neither did the firm's ER Mod).

MONEY SAVERS

⬇ Verify Your Factors

If your company has been accident free, identify your industry's legally mandated ballast factor. Are you being charged the minimum workers' compensation premium? If not, why not?

⬇ Question All Costs

If your company is paying the legal minimum, it is reasonable to question the additional expenses you incur from safety consultants, hot new training programs, and similar other measures. If it ain't broke, why pay to fix it?

⬇ Investigate Third-Party Involvement

Sometimes a third party is responsible or partially responsible for an on-the-job injury. A lawsuit filed by an injured employee or workers' compensation carrier against the third party can help offset claim costs and thus minimize negative impacts on an employer's ER Mod. Typical third-party claims involve motor vehicle accidents, product liability, and personal or professional liability.

CLAIM RESERVES

High claim payouts increase your firm's experience modifier and thus your workers' compensation premiums. High *claim re-*

serves (amounts levied against your account to cover payouts a carrier *may* have to make on a past, unresolved claim) have the same effect.

Claim Reserves: A Problem for Employers

Workers' compensation is insurance for employers. A claim reserve is essentially insurance for carriers. Claim reserves allow a carrier to collect additional monies from a policyholder to cover potential but unanticipated problems relative to an existing (but unresolved) claim.

Claim reserves are a major profit center for carriers, yet they remain a mystery to most policyholders. It is imperative that you understand the damage a claim reserve can do to your company's finances. Consider the following scenarios:

Scenario 1 Jackie is hurt at work but recovers quickly and completely. It costs the workers' compensation carrier $500 to close his claim. The claim has a negligible impact on his employer's experience modifier and premiums. *Note:* In some states, Jackie's employer could have paid the $500 itself and saved any workers' compensation complications.

Scenario 2 Jackie is hurt at work and appears to recover quickly and completely. His employer's compensation carrier pays $500 in medical expenses but does *not* close Jackie's claim. It decides that he *may* incur further expenses (medical, time loss, rehabilitation, etc.) to the tune of, say, $20,000. *Note:* The carrier doesn't necessarily expect to pay any additional expenses; it just believes the potential is there. The $20,000 is charged against the employer's account as a claim reserve. *This claim reserve, until removed, has the same negative impact on the firm's experience modifier as a $20,000 claim.* In other words, the employer is severely penalized for something that probably will not happen. The workers' compensation carrier receives a substantial what-if windfall even though it never pays more than $500 on John's claim.

Minimizing Claim Reserve Damage

There are two ways to minimize the financial impact of claim reserves: (1) avoid allowing claims to be categorized as time-loss accidents and (2) evaluate all claim reserves. Never accept a claim reserve without question (or answers).

Claim reserves are made only against time-loss injuries; therefore, you should know your state's legal definition of time loss and do whatever you can to keep on-the job accidents from qualifying. For example, in some states, an injury is not a time-loss injury until the victim has missed at least three days of work. In these states, businesses should do whatever they can to get injured workers back on the job prior to this legal definition deadline. They can:

1. Offer the injured employee light duty (book training, nonphysical or less strenuous tasks, office or committee work, a modified job site, etc.).
2. Offer the injured employee longer breaks.
3. Schedule the employee's medical appointments on company time.
4. Send the employee home early but "on the clock."

Of course, no action should ever be taken that puts an injured worker's health at additional risk. That would be morally (and economically) insupportable.

You should close workers' compensation claims as soon as possible. Claim reserves are removed from accounts as soon as their associated claims are settled and medically closed.

To effect a medical closure, a physician must sign a release stating that (1) the accident victim can return to full duty, (2) he is medically stationary with no permanent disabilities, and (3) the risk of reinjury due to the original injury is small or nonexistent.

If closing a claim would be premature and a claim reserve appears appropriate, ensure that the amount levied is reasonable. Does the claim reserve seem excessive given the injury? Ask the carrier for a breakdown and explanation of the amount levied. If the assessment still seems excessive, have it reviewed by medical or legal consultants. If necessary, they can help argue for a removal of (or a reduction in) the claim reserve.

Bottom line, claim reserves are often assessed without sufficient justification. Why? Because (1) they protect the carrier, (2) the carrier has the ability to assess them, (3) they make the carrier money, and (4) policyholders don't track them. High reserves can and should be challenged, medically or legally.

MONEY SAVERS

⬇ Facilitate Medical Appointments

Timely medical appointments are critical to quick claim closure. Many companies are using company doctors (or contracted clinics) to facilitate employee and business schedules and needs. These medical providers can determine how quickly an employer can return to work and what restrictions, if any, should apply.

⬇ Monitor Changes in Employment Status

Keep close tabs on any injured employee who decides to quit before his claim is closed. Schedule a medical appointment for the employee on company time, and go with him to facilitate matters. Ask if the attending physician will issue a medical release. If possible, the release should be signed by the employee. Once the injured worker has left your employ, it is more difficult for you to manage the workers' compensation process. If the injured worker has already quit, your company lawyers should approach him about a claim release. If you have reason to believe that he may pursue a false or exaggerated claim, inform your lawyer and compensation carrier immediately. A private investigator may be hired to document the ex-employee's physical abilities.

⬇ Review Your Reserves

Keep a tickler file to remind you to review all claim reserves at least ninety days before your policy renewal date. This gives you three months to get all of the outstanding claims closed and the reserves removed. If the reserves are removed before your policy renews, they won't affect the premium.

⬇ Verify All Information

Carefully and continually monitoring claim reserves, job classifications, and experience modifiers will lead to ongoing cost savings. Many businesses pay unnecessarily high workers' compensation premiums because their policies and claim figures are based on inaccurate information.

Multistate Coverage

Employers who conduct business in more than one state must be careful to ensure that their employees are always covered (thus avoiding penalties, fines, shutdowns, costly out-of-pocket accidents, etc.) and they are purchasing the cheapest workers' compensation coverage available.

Reciprocal Agreements

Some state regulations allow for *extraterritorial* workers' compensation coverage—that is, current coverage that can be carried to another state. Never assume partial or total reciprocity between states.

Extraterritorial issues are complex. State rules must be checked monthly (they constantly change). See the sample state exterritoriality statute in Resources and Checklists Section C.

In some states, extraterritorial coverage is based on the number of days a specific employee works in the secondary state; in other states, this coverage depends on the number of days a second-state work site is open. Some states (including Hawaii and Colorado) will not accept extraterritorial coverage *even for sales calls or other short-term work* (consider the impact *that* could have on planning sales conferences!). All construction workers in Nevada must have Nevada coverage. The list goes on and on. Before an employee even enters another state, you should check with that state's workers' compensation officials to determine if he is in fact "working" in that state. Before conducting business in a new state, you must:

1. Inform your current carrier and workers' compensation attorney.
2. Inform the new state.
3. Determine if extraterritorial coverage is acceptable (given your business parameters).
4. If necessary, purchase coverage in the new state.
5. Determine which state's laws—your home state's or the second state's—would cover an injury.

Obtaining Workers' Compensation Coverage

Individual states determine who can sell workers' compensation coverage inside their borders. Policies are (1) sold only by the state, (2) sold by private companies at rates set by the state, or (3) sold by private companies at market rates.

State agencies can supply a list of approved workers' compensation providers (unless the state has a monopoly on the sales end). When selecting a carrier, consider the following:

▼ Pure premiums (the providers' premium per $100 payroll in your industry)
▼ Potential discounts (based on volume, safety records, experience modifiers, etc.)
▼ Customer assistance or communication programs (e.g., does the carrier quickly inform customers when state workers' compensation rules change?)

MONEY SAVERS

⬇ Obtain Group Discounts

Investigate membership affiliation discounts in every state in which your company does business. The year one of the authors joined a statewide employers' association, he saved 19 percent on his workers' compensation premiums—this in addition to the discounts received as a function of his individual ratings.

⬇ Leverage Extraterritoriality

Investigate exterritoriality agreements carefully. You may be able to purchase inexpensive insurance in one state that will cover your employees in another.

⬇ Use Strategic Staffing

Strategic staffing or scheduling may reduce your workers' compensation costs. For example, if your company does minimal business in a second state, consider handling that territory through temporary or contract workers, teleconferencing, or some other means. Do not allow traveling sales personnel to spend so many consecutive days in a neighboring state that you have to buy additional compensation policies.

USING OUTSIDERS AND SPECIALISTS

It is possible to minimize workers' compensation exposure by minimizing the number of people you employ. Using outside specialists to handle extremely dangerous work or outside generalists to handle extremely routine work is a cost- (and safety-) effective strategy.

Subcontracting

Everyday tasks should be handled by company personnel. Unusual (e.g., risky) jobs are best performed by specialty subcontractors. They have the training, experience, and equipment necessary to minimize on-the-job accidents.

Subcontracting dangerous tasks has two major benefits: (1)

it keeps untrained employees out of harm's way, and (2) it insulates your company's experience modifier (any accidents accrue to the subcontractor's workers' compensation account).

Note: This is not a "protect mine, sacrifice his" morality play. Sometimes a dangerous task needs to be performed. In accordance with common sense, it should be done by experts (the subcontractor's employees) rather than novices (your regular staff). Subcontracting dangerous tasks creates a win-win business situation.

When to Use Subcontracting

- ▾ Your workers don't have the experience necessary to perform the work in a safe manner.
- ▾ Your employees don't have the equipment required to do the job safely (or economically).
- ▾ Your staff doesn't have a working knowledge of the task's recommended safety procedures.
- ▾ Your company doesn't intend to continue doing this line of work.
- ▾ The dangerous task is an occasional one.

Always ask subcontractors to provide proof of workers' compensation coverage. You don't want their injured employees to look toward your compensation or liability policies for financial remuneration.

Temporary Help

Temporary help can come in handy. Unlike seasonal or part-time workers, temps are hired by an employment agency and subsequently leased to other companies. Temporary workers are best used on routine, relatively safe tasks.

Temp workers can help reduce workers' compensation costs in three ways:

1. By replacing tired or overworked employees, temps can help your employees avoid careless injuries.
2. Temps can perform routine tasks, leaving your highly

trained (and high-wage) employees to handle specialized or dangerous jobs.

3. Your company's experience modifier is not affected when and if a temp is injured. A temp's claim is charged against the employment agency.

Note: Like subcontractors, temps are not cannon fodder. Subcontractors should perform unusual, high-risk tasks; temps should be used for traditional, low-risk jobs. This allows your company to maximize the use of its trained personnel while minimizing its workers' compensation costs and exposure.

MONEY SAVERS

⬇ Investigate Your Subcontractors

Ask the subcontractor or temp agency about its own experience modifier. Look for companies with a safe track record. A careless subcontractor or temp worker may hurt someone else (someone on *your* payroll and compensation account).

⬇ Smooth the Transition

Be aware of potential personnel problems associated with using temp help. Temps can generate anger among full-time and part-time workers because they often reduce the need for overtime work (that is, overtime *pay*). They tend to get the "easy jobs." They may be viewed as potential replacements (particularly if the firm has recently experienced a downsizing). Be prepared to show your workers how they will benefit from temp help. For example, temporary workers can help the firm lower its accident rates (as a function of less stressed and pressed workers), reduce mandatory overtime, and lead to more efficient deployment of trained personnel.

4

Employee Involvement and Training

Employees should be involved in all facets of developing, implementing, promoting, maintaining, and administering your corporate safety program. In the long run, ongoing employee involvement saves money and lives.

Studies show a strong causal relationship between employee involvement and high morale. Workers with high morale have fewer on-the-job accidents and injuries. They file fewer workers' compensation claims. The claims they generate are smaller and involve less time loss. They do not attempt to defraud the company (or condone others who do).

In summary, keeping your employees happy and involved will help you reduce your workers' compensation costs.

OCCUPATIONAL SAFETY AND HEALTH COMMITTEES

Occupational safety and health committees are dictated by both law and common sense. Safety committees, which ideally include both management and hourly employees, oversee all workplace safety and health issues. OSHA Act regulations regarding these formal committees are extensive and detailed.

The Goal of the Safety Committee

The purpose of a safety committee is to bring workers and management together in a nonadversarial, cooperative effort to promote safety and health in the workplace. The committee helps the employer by making recommendations for change regarding occupational safety and health issues.

The key to a good and effective safety committee is extensive and legitimate employee involvement. Safety committees make many decisions that directly affect the entire workforce. Lower-level workers are more likely to accept, promote, and abide by a committee decision if they had in role in making it.

Sometimes it can be difficult for a safety committee to find employee volunteers. People don't want to help validate Gourd's Axiom (a committee meeting is an event in which the minutes are kept and the hours are lost).

Still, employee participation is crucial to this mandated process. If no employees volunteer for your safety committee, document all formal and informal recruitment efforts and then appoint qualified employees to the open positions. Identify why employees are apathetic. If they believe their input would be useless or ignored, your business has an entirely different—and perhaps worse—problem than apathy. Consider making safety committee membership a required function of certain jobs.

Developing a Successful Safety Committee

There are four steps in developing and maintaining a successful Safety Committee: laying the foundation, deciding membership issues, forming the committee, and conducting meetings. All of these steps have a legal and logical basis.

Step 1: Lay the Foundation

1. *Identify the appropriate federal or state occupational safety and health regulations.* For example, is your company so small that no safety committee is required? Or will you have to form a separate safety committee for every facility or job site?

2. *Include information regarding the safety committee in the company policy statement.* For example, explain why the committee was established; the roles and responsibilities of the committee, the company managers, supervisors, and hourly employees; and the cooperation and support required companywide. Including a formal statement of support from the CEO is also a good idea.

3. *Communicate safety committee information to all employees.* This can be done through a number of avenues: memos, group meetings, one-on-one contact, public address systems, newsletters, bulletin boards, brochures or flyers, company handbooks.

Step 2: Decide Membership Issues

1. *Determine the appropriate number of committee members.* There should be at least one representative from each major work area (more if a particular area has a disproportionate number of close calls or on-the-job injuries). Ideally, half of the committee members will be managers, and half will be hourly workers.

2. *Stagger terms to ensure a continuing level of knowledge and competence.* To quickly establish workplace credibility, and facilitate term staggering, start managers with the shortest terms and stress to hourly workers that their experience is particularly valuable.

3. *Identify potential committee members.* Employer representatives can be appointed; employee representatives should be elected or chosen from among volunteers. Ideally, the safety committee members will be dedicated to preventing injury and illness accidents; be interested in serving on the committee; have good people and communication skills; have a high level of cred-

ibility, experience, and knowledge; and be able to get things done through and with other people.

4. *Add relatively new employees to the safety committee.* They often have intriguing and insightful questions about why a status quo works the way it does—important questions that conditioned veterans would not think to ask.

5. *Quickly notify safety committee members and then the company at large of their appointment.* Make sure that employee supervisors, the personnel department, and the payroll department take any necessary steps to support the assignment.

6. *Send all members the committee rules, parameters, meeting schedules, time lines, membership lists, long-term agendas, and any other important information.* Introductory safety committee training should be conducted.

Step 3: Form the Committee

1. *Ensure that the safety committee has a solid structure.* Does it have clearly defined purposes and goals? Does it have realistic and measurable objectives and completion dates? Is the committee's authority clear? Do the committee members understand their roles, responsibilities, functions, and duties? Does the committee have a process for accepting formal and informal employee input? Does the company have a system for taking, filing, and distributing (privately or publicly) the minutes?

2. *Ensure that the safety committee has a basic action plan.* What are the committee's communication channels? What kind of tracking, record-keeping, and reporting system does it need? How often will it meet? Who will develop and route meeting agendas (ideally three to five days prior to each meeting)? How will the committee ensure that its decisions mesh with health and safety regulations?

Step 4: Conduct Meetings

1. *Ensure that the safety committee follows good meeting etiquette.* For example, meetings should begin and end on time, minutes of the previous meeting should be read and approved,

the agenda should be followed, and any past decisions should be reviewed.

2. *Ensure that committee members have the knowledge and training necessary to perform their legal duties.* They need to be familiar with health and safety regulations, aware of the company's specific workplace hazards, knowledgeable about accident and incident investigation principles, and know where and how to find information regarding new developments in personal protective equipment, safety technology, and other relevant issues.

3. *Develop a system for feedback.* To determine if the committee is performing adequately, ask these questions: Did every committee member receive an agenda and minutes in a timely manner? Did everyone contribute to the discussion? Do committee members understand their legal and safety duties? Were there problems releasing the employee representatives from their duties? Did the payroll department adequately handle any related overtime or travel expenses? Did representatives come to the meeting prepared?

Note: The safety committee should not be expected to critique what it accomplishes. That job is better left to managers and other employees. This feedback step should center on how well the committee itself functions.

MONEY SAVERS

⬇ Promote "Off the Job" Safety

Safety committees can also make suggestions to employees relative to off-the-job safety. A committee might suggest, for instance, that employees wear seat belts even when they are driving on their own time, or it could publish information relative to safe ladder usage in the company newsletter. Why bother? Because:

▾ An employee who does things safely at home is less likely to do them inappropriately at work. You can help employees develop good habits.

- ▼ Morale improves when employees realize that the company cares about them twenty-four hours a day. They feel less expendable.
- ▼ Reducing off-the-job injuries minimizes the odds that an injured employee will show up to work and pretend that his injury happened on the job.
- ▼ Injuries both on and off the job have a negative impact on staffing, overall productivity, medical leave and expenses, and morale.

⬇ Consider Committee Costs

Delegate safety committee functions to the member who can perform them (or have them performed by a subordinate) at the lowest cost. It often makes sense to have the committee itself chaired by an hourly employee. This improves the average worker's image of the committee and also decreases management costs.

TRAINING STAFF FOR SAFETY

Realistically, your safety program is only as good as your training program. While the OSHA Act does not address or mandate training as a stand-alone subject, dozens of its specialized regulations contain individual training requirements.

The Successful Training Program

A successful training program provides the appropriate level and kind of training in the appropriate subjects to the appropriate employees at the appropriate time. Of course, it should also meet (and document that it meets) any applicable OSHA Act mandates.

To support this training goal, the program should meet a number of objectives. It needs to be well planned and organized, thorough, continual, and self-reinforcing (do the employees use what they learn?). You should also ensure that the company keeps careful documentation of its training efforts. This information facilitates program and expense evaluation and provides a legal defense against negligence in the event of an on-the-job injury. While OSHA can provide training guidelines, it is important to recognize that these guidelines (except where specifically mandated by statute) are not mandatory; nor are they total or complete. A business that follows them completely may still find itself in violation of the General Duty Clause. Nevertheless, using OSHA guidelines when developing parts of your corporate training plan will work in your favor if you are ever called before the OSHA Review Commission.

Components of the Training Program

OSHA training guidelines recommend the following components in a training program: a training audit, determination of need, need identification, defining goals and objectives, developing and conducting training activities, and evaluating and improving the program.

Training programs should be designed by experts in the field. Yes, it's expensive, but not nearly as expensive as ongoing safety problems. To be successful, a training program must be designed in a linear fashion. Don't try to put the cart before the horse.

Step 1: Conduct a Safety Audit

A safety audit is essentially an objective observation of where the company stands now. It is important that your expert:

1. *Audit every job description in every department.* Identify every job task, its related hazards (materials, equipment, etc.), and what is being done to eliminate or minimize them.

2. *Observe every employee.* Determine if new employees were properly trained, transferred employees have the appropriate training for their new jobs, and all employees use personal pro-

tective equipment properly (a high percentage of OSHA citations are given for these three failings).

3. *Make sure the audit is comprehensive.* Every department should be audited by at least two people: the general safety expert and a specific task expert (department supervisor, lead worker, etc.).

4. *Analyze the work site,* with the intention of changing and improving areas where the audit identified shortfalls.

At this stage, the goal is to document your company's current position. Resist the urge to validate, explain, or cover any shortfalls. You need to know where you are before you can determine where you need to go.

Step 2: Determine Training Needs

Next, determine if there is a need for new or different training relative to general health or safety rules, specific work guidelines, and OSHA Act mandates. *Note:* An accident or near-miss incident usually indicates a need for more or better training.

It is important that you recognize what training can and cannot do. As part of the overall safety program, training can effectively address problems resulting from:

- ▾ A lack of knowledge or understanding
- ▾ Unfamiliarity with a new job, materials, or equipment
- ▾ Incorrect performance of a task
- ▾ Employee motivation or awareness problems

The OSHA Act requires training and knowledge relative to numerous important safety issues. These include:

- ▾ Accident prevention signs
- ▾ Anhydrous ammonia
- ▾ Bloodborne pathogens
- ▾ Cranes
- ▾ Construction
- ▾ Electrical safety-related work practices

- ▼ Employee emergency plans and fire prevention plans
- ▼ Energy control (lockout/tagout)
- ▼ Fixed extinguishing systems
- ▼ Flammable and combustible liquid tank storage
- ▼ Hazard communication
- ▼ HAZWOPER (hazardous waste and emergency response plans)
- ▼ Mechanical power presses
- ▼ Noise exposure
- ▼ Permit-confined spaces
- ▼ Portable fire extinguishers
- ▼ Powered industrial trucks
- ▼ Process safety management
- ▼ Servicing of single-piece and multipiece rims and wheels
- ▼ Storage and handling of liquefied petroleum gases
- ▼ Telecommunications
- ▼ Ventilation
- ▼ Welding
- ▼ Woodworking machinery

For additional information see the self-inspection checklists in Resources and Checklists Section H.

Step 3: Identify Training Needs

Your expert will need to identify the specific training that is needed. This involves analyzing each job to identify what employees need to know to perform it safely and effectively and determining whether employees know what they need to know. For assistance in Step 3, your expert may choose to:

- ▼ Study old accident records to determine where problems occur.
- ▼ Directly observe employees performing their jobs.
- ▼ Evaluate training programs run by others in the industry.
- ▼ Ask every employee to describe his job in detail, both subjectively and objectively.

Pay particular attention to tasks employees describe as being confusing, frustrating, frightening, risky, or not liked. These comments generally identify problem areas.

Step 4: Define Goals and Objectives

Your consultant will help you identify training goals and objectives that define what employees should do, do better, or stop doing, Ideally, these objectives will be:

- ▾ written
- ▾ clear
- ▾ action oriented
- ▾ specific and sufficiently detailed
- ▾ measurable

Once the goals and objectives are identified, realize that the employee should be able to demonstrate that he can meet or has met them. Even good objectives can be poorly worded, as this example shows:

Poorly worded objective: "The employee should be careful when using Equipment A."

More accurate and complete: "Before using Equipment A, the employee will understand how this equipment functions, know when and how it should be used, and successfully complete (and sign off on) Training for Equipment A."

Step 5: Develop and Conduct Training Activities

There is no perfect way to train employees. Your expert will have to design a custom program that meets the specific needs of your workers. It may include on-the-job training, on-site classroom work, community college courses (with expenses reimbursed by the company), self-study courses, lectures, mentoring, or something else. In general, try to develop a training program that will:

▼ Motivate your employees by answering the question, "What's in it for me?" (greater personal safety, higher skill level, promotability, greater productivity or pay, etc.).
▼ Include written materials for later reference.
▼ Be linear (teach procedures in the order in which they are performed).
▼ Simulate the actual job task and conditions.
▼ Be appropriate to the job type (e.g., teaching physical skills requires a different kind of training from teaching mental ones).
▼ Include a feedback function (can the employee prove that he has learned what he needed to learn?).

Step 6: Evaluate and Improve the Program

Analyzing employee feedback, supervisors' observations, and workplace improvements is important. Listen to what employees have to say about the training program. Look for and analyze changes in the company safety record. Compare your safety record to those of others in your industry. You and the safety expert should ask some tough questions. The two most important:

1. Was any of the training redundant, confusing, distracting, or missing?
2. What did the employees learn or fail to learn?

MONEY SAVERS

⬇ Analyze Training Needs Carefully

There are two schools of thought: (1) training is cheap and (2) training is expensive. Both are right. To minimize both costs and safety risks, carefully analyze which employees need the most training. Those employee populations with the highest level of risk should receive the most training or the most expensive forms of training. Training mandated by the OSHA Act is a top priority.

⬇ Coordinate Departments

Your personnel and safety departments should work together to coordinate training programs. Too often, a "this is my turf" attitude causes different departments to reinvent or repeat the wheel.

FORMAL TRAINING PROGRAMS

Several major safety programs are mandated and tightly controlled by the OSHA Act. The following overview will ensure that your specific programs contain the necessary safety and communication components.

Hazardous Substances Program

The hazardous substances program protects employees who use hazardous substances (chemicals, gases, etc.) in the workplace. The program must include rule familiarization, hazard assessment, written guidelines for hazardous substance use, employee training, and program evaluation. These programs tend to be very long and detailed in nature.

A hazardous substance program is employee oriented, but employers can also benefit from its proper application. For example, they can use it to get and keep their workers' attention; awareness promotes safety. They can also use the written program and guidelines as a checklist for informing or training employees and as a starting place for program evaluation, feedback, and expert analysis.

An effective hazardous substances program will have all of the following components:

▼ A written hazardous substance program readily available to all employees.

▼ A written list of all hazardous chemicals present in the workplace.

▼ A system for updating lists when new chemicals are present at the workplace.

▼ The current Material Safety Data Sheets on all hazardous substances.

▼ A system for ensuring new substances come with MSDS and labels.

▼ A system for ensuring that secondary containers have safety and warning labels.

▼ A program that ensures all outside contractors have hazardous substance information.

▼ An extensive training program that covers such topics as:
  —Hazardous communication rules (legal and company specific)
  —Chemical types (solvents, corrosives, etc.) and their associated hazards
  —Gas types and their associated hazards
  —Routine task hazards
  —Unique hazards (chemicals in pipes, working in confined spaces)
  —Where gases or chemicals are stored and used
  —MSDSs and warning and safety labels
  —How to detect and respond to the presence or release of hazardous substances
  —Proper work practices
  —Proper personal protective equipment
  —Proper first aid techniques

Hazardous Communication Program

The OSHA Act's hazardous communication standard is designed to alert employees about workplace chemicals by giving them greater access to information on the physical and health hazards of chemicals, safe handling precautions, and emergency first aid procedures. It covers all industries, including the construction industry, in which employees are exposed to hazardous chemicals.

A hazardous communication program works hand in hand with the hazardous substances program, making the latter seem real to employees. You can't have an efficient and effective safety program unless employees know about it. The standard requires employers to set up hazard communication programs that include:

- Label on Containers
- MSDSs
- Training Programs

Hazardous Task Identification

The goal of the hazardous task identification plan is to identify and eliminate and otherwise control work site components that present a potential danger to employees. It is the "potential danger" parameter that makes this process so complex. Every hazardous task identification program should include a basic hazard survey, hazard guidelines, routine self-inspections, and employee training.

Potential dangers can be physical in nature; others could be cynically classified as dangerous in terms of company image, internal politics, or union relations. Try to identify inherent hazards, potential hazards, and systemic hazards (situations that, rightly or wrongly, could result in a workers' compensation claim) in regard to accidents or illnesses.

To identify hazards:

- Obtain relevant OSHA Act regulations and guidelines.
- Gather information on generally recognized safe work practices.
- Look for physical hazards of all types (e.g., stairs).
- Audit hazardous materials, equipment, tools, and so forth.
- Evaluate employee work habits (e.g., do workers clean up spills immediately?).

▾ Discuss safety problems and concerns with all employees and subcontractors.

▾ Use anonymous suggestion boxes with guaranteed follow-up.

To identify specific areas of need, review:

▾ Accident, injury, or illness data.
▾ Workers' compensation claims.
▾ Areas of high turnover or absenteeism.
▾ Information on past safety, health, and training programs.
▾ Company policy statements.
▾ Work, health, and safety rules.
▾ Guidelines for proper work practices and procedures.

Implement work site self-inspections that are performed regularly. Their frequency will depend on:

▾ The operations involved.
▾ How dangerous the task is.
▾ Employee abilities (can employees carry out the inspections?).
▾ Changes in equipment or work processes.
▾ The history of workplace injuries and illnesses.
▾ Their effectiveness (done by experts who know OSHA Act requirements).

Consider minimizing or eliminating hazardous tasks by:

▾ Subcontracting or outsourcing.
▾ Using outside delivery services.
▾ Limiting employee access.
▾ Substitution of materials.
▾ Specialized training.

It is not our intent to propose simply moving the hazard elsewhere; however, other organizations may (as a function of their employee training, experience, specialized equipment, etc.) be better equipped to handle hazardous tasks.

Personal Protective Equipment

A good personal protective equipment (PPE) program will identify inherent workplace hazards, the PPE capable of minimizing or eliminating them, and the education and training of all employees.

Keep in mind that although personal protective equipment is required by law and has saved a great many lives and limbs, it is no panacea. Even a good PPE program does not take the place of good workplace design and safe practices. Work sites and tasks designed with safety in mind can eliminate problems; PPE can only minimize and perhaps, in some cases, exacerbate them. For example, the National Institute for Occupational Safety and Health (a subset of the U.S. Centers for Disease Control and Prevention) recently announced that it was "unable to find any evidence that wearing back belts reduces the risk of back injury among healthy workers." In addition, Director Linda Rosenstock suggested that these belts may increase the risk of injury by encouraging workers to lift more weight than they should.

Your personal protective equipment program must, as a minimum, address inherent workplace hazards, PPE capable of minimizing or eliminating these hazards, and the education and training of all employees. Employees need to know the following:

- ▼ When is PPE necessary?
- ▼ What PPE is necessary?
- ▼ How should PPE be put on, taken off, adjusted, and worn?
- ▼ What can specific PPE do and not do?
- ▼ What is the proper care, maintenance, useful life, and disposal of specific PPE?

Employee acceptance and use of PPE can be maximized by these guidelines:

1. Let employees make the final PPE selection (brand, style, etc.).
2. The company should pay for some (preferably all) of the PPE.
3. Use employee horror stories to promote PPE.
4. Continually demonstrate your company's commitment to PPE.
5. Visually demonstrate why PPE is important.
6. Ensure that all employees read and understand the company's program.
7. Have employees sign, and then insist that they follow, their safety contract.

Note: Under the OSHA Act, you must ensure that all PPE (even that owned by employees) is adequate, properly maintained, and sanitized. Company-owned PPE is easier to inspect and control.

Lockout/Tagout Programs

Lockout/tagout programs are essentially machine disability programs. The lockout component ensures that equipment that is being maintained or serviced is not accidentally turned on. The tagout component ensures that questionable equipment is not accidentally used.

Designing a successful lockout/tagout program has three steps:

1. Identify relevant federal and state OSHA Act regulations.
2. Define when, where, why, and what lockout and tagout actions are required.
3. Develop employee training programs.

Because lockout/tagout programs have a very visual component (e.g., padlocks on energy sources, large and colorful DO NOT OPERATE tags), cost-conscious businesspeople are also using these programs to build employee awareness, communicate the concern their business has for safety, and improve employee morale. Bottom line, a lockout/tagout situation is a clear demonstration to employees of how important their safety is to you and your business.

When establishing a lockout program, review specific types of energy to be shut down, procedures for the control of hazardous energy vis à vis shutdown, equipment isolation, release of stored energy, verification of isolation, and anything else that is necessary. Your written lockout/tagout program should address the following:

- Who is responsible for lockout and tagout issues
- Who can lock out or tag out equipment
- Who can end the lockout/tagout of equipment
- What equipment and tools are covered by the lockout/tagout
- What energy sources and concerns are covered by the lockout/tagout
- When lockout/tagout must be used
- How lockout/tagout must be used
- Specific lockout/tagout devices (padlocks, visual tags, chains, etc.)
- How equipment and tools are tagged out
- Lockout/tagout awareness and training
- Periodic inspections

FORMAL AND INFORMAL SAFETY MEETINGS

Safety must be a pervasive part of your organizational culture. It should be a consistent and persistent corporate theme. Safety information should be distributed through both formal and informal meetings. This combination of communication methods will make sure you get your safety message across.

Formal Safety Lectures

Formal safety lectures are an excellent communication tool. Because of their reproducibility, low expense, and ease of documentation, they are a staple of corporate safety programs.

Formal safety lectures are often considered a subset of general training, but there are major differences between training programs and formal safety lectures. Formal safety lectures should last no longer than twenty minutes, and they should cover a single subject. They are more informational than hands-on. Employees may see them as less threatening, less important, and more boring than "training." Formal safety lectures are best used when:

▼ The company needs or wants to document the communication of safety information.
▼ Consistency in the presentation is vital.
▼ Specific information needs to be addressed (e.g., explaining general or specific job hazards and risks, discussing or reviewing proper usage of equipment, maintaining awareness of safety issues).
▼ The process will be repeated on a regular basis for new or retrained employees or for different departments.
▼ The information can be supplemented or supported (e.g., with handouts, charts, audiovisual materials, videos).

Informal Safety Meetings

While formal safety lectures are one way in nature (from the lecturer to the listener), informal safety meetings provide two-way communication. Thus, they are both an important informational and a crucial feedback tool.

Informal meetings of all kinds are designed to solicit employee-based information and feedback. Like a cat, a business has many lives. A business with fifty employees has fifty lives' worth of expertise, experience, and expectations. It's a knowledge base that money can't buy, and it comes free with every employee. Smart businesspeople are quick to access this asset. Informal safety meetings can be broken down into standard meetings and tailgate meetings.

Standard Safety Meetings

Standard safety meetings address a variety of safety concerns and are usually conducted near, but not at, the work area. Conference rooms and cafeterias are common sites.

One standard meeting format, the *feedback forum,* is designed to accentuate the positive. Employees are asked about streamlining or improving their jobs, safety issues, how certain situations were handled by former employers, or how they would change their job sites. Supervisors can pick a topic and encourage employees to come to the next meeting with related ideas or concerns.

Foul-up forums provide another helpful format. Employees are asked to talk about their mistakes; by doing so, they are able to educate others. To encourage input, some companies offer rewards for anecdotes. Employees must not be penalized for coming clean. The goal of the meeting is to educate, not castigate.

Note: Employees are often reluctant to share information with management. This failure to communicate is often a function of the *F* word: *fear.* Employees don't talk to their supervisors because they're afraid of being ridiculed, reprimanded, or replaced. Never penalize employees for educating their managers! Safety input must be solicited, accepted, valued, and used.

Standard safety meetings are best used when:

- ▾ The company wishes to encourage employee participation.
- ▾ The company needs to gather information or ideas.
- ▾ The company wants to discuss options with employees (e.g., which brand of personal protective equipment the employees prefer).
- ▾ The company wishes to involve employees in minor safety or job decisions.

Two ongoing issues at safety meetings should be (1) how the company can reduce work site stress and (2) how it can provide positive reinforcement to its employees. Addressing these two subjects is important. Although they are seldom seen as safety issues, numerous studies indicate that positive reinforcement and lower levels of stress have a direct correlation to work site safety. Safety meetings are a quick, easy, and efficient way to broach these subjects.

You may also want to conduct regularly scheduled employee surveys to measure and document the stress individual workers feel. Consider what happened to two employers who terminated employees:

> They [two employees] went to file unemployment claims, as was their due. While in line they were approached by a lawyer who promised them, "I can get you a better deal than hanging around here will." Charging post termination stress, the employees filed multi-thousand dollar claims against their employer. . . .
>
> An employee of another small company, in anticipation of being fired, brought in a lawyer while he was still at work to establish grounds for job related stress. The employer countered by bringing in a doctor, who refuted the allegation by issuing the employee a clean bill of health. The two specialists canceled each other out. "After a lot of wrangling back and forth," says the business's owner, "all that happened was that our insurance premiums went up."[1]

Informal safety meetings should include a quick reminder to workers of the benefits and programs available to employees. Employees can't use a benefit or program unless they know about it. Ongoing awareness of positive company programs (and the high morale it creates) is critical to safety success.

Tailgate Meetings

Tailgate meetings are convened on the job site to discuss specific hazards of that site. They are based on the premise that some work hazards do not become apparent until the supervisors and employees are actually at the work site. Such hazards could include excess traffic, standing water, or overhead work being performed on scaffolding or a roof.

Tailgate meetings are used to identify, list, and discuss job hazards and hazard elimination or minimization. They are brief, to the point, and—in the case of certain work sites—required by

[1]Robert A. Mamis, "Employees from Hell," *Inc.* (January 1995).

the OSHA Act. Extensive documentation is not necessary, although the supervisor should date and record tailgate meetings in his files. An ounce of documentation is worth a pound of penalties.

MONEY SAVER

⬇ **Encourage Employee Ownership**

Give employees a stake in safety meetings by allowing employees to run them. Their lead will help you to focus quickly and inexpensively on issues that the employees feel need attention.

5

Handling Accidents and Injuries

Your business should have a before, during, and after attitude toward on-the-job accidents.

Before an accident occurs, take steps to avoid problems and educate your hourly employees and supervisors so that they can handle an accident efficiently, effectively, and humanely.

During the accident investigation phase, be prepared to care for the injured employee, document and verify the incident, and process the necessary paperwork (internal files, workers' compensation claim, any required legal notifications, etc.).

After an accident or claim is wrapped up, determine what went wrong and what can be done to prevent recurrences.

BEFORE THE ACCIDENT

Education and awareness can help your company avoid and/or minimize on-the-job injuries. Supervisors and employees need to know what to do in the event of an accident, and they need to know how to identify accidents waiting to happen. In terms of attitude, always be ready for accidents; always be in a state of physical and mental preparedness.

Preparing the Workforce

Supervisors and employees should know exactly what they are required to do in the event of an accident. Guidelines should be written and widely distributed. Individuals should receive responsiveness training appropriate to their levels of responsibility and specific work site needs.

Education is crucial to reducing workers' compensation costs. Supervisors and employees have different responsibilities in the event of an accident. Prior to an accident, they must know what these responsibilities are. As a condition of their initial and continuing employment, employees must formally agree to:

1. Immediately report any accidents or near misses to their supervisor.
2. Follow any appropriate emergency action plan.
3. Cooperate fully during any accident investigation.
4. Immediately report any suspicions they may have relative to a workers' compensation claim.
5. Report any off-the-job accidents or medical conditions that will affect their ability to do the job.

Many people have difficulty responding appropriately in an emergency. By simplifying what they need to do, you increase the odds that they will be able to do it. For example, individuals (or a pair of individuals) can be assigned specific tasks.

For legal reasons, supervisors should always be responsible for determining medical actions. For example, employee 1 may be responsible for notifying the safety manager; employee 2 may be responsible for clearing the area.

An emergency checklist can also help employees focus on, and complete, critical tasks. It is particularly important that employees be given training and information about how to deal with AIDS. Workers must know how to handle blood on the work site, prevent disease transmission, and understand other precautions. Just as HIV-positive workers have a right to medical privacy, all workers have a right to safety information.

Note: Do not suggest that an employee will suffer by making an honest report. Make it clear that with the attending physician's help and approval, you intend to help the employee with such things as job modifications, light duty, and temporary reassignment. These needs and responsibilities should be discussed with employees on a regular basis and presented in positive terms. All you really want employees to do when there is an accident is report it immediately and help rather than hinder. Stress why doing these two things is in their best interests and in the best interests of their coworkers.

What you need from supervisors is more structural (record information, gather documentation, prepare paperwork, etc.) than attitudinal in nature. When an accident is reported, the supervisor's responsibilities (discussed later in this chapter) can be arduous and exacting.

As the employer, it is your responsibility to educate your employees and supervisors about what they are to do in the event of an accident. Teach them to swim before they go off the deep end.

Ongoing Accident Avoidance

Due to new equipment, materials, personnel, work site conditions, even well-designed jobs and facilities can evolve into trouble spots. Employers and employees should always be on the lookout for dangerous workplace characteristics.

An employee or supervisor should regularly walk through the job site searching for dangerous job characteristics.

The Most Common Work Site Hazards

▼ Requiring employees to regularly or repetitively twist, wring, bend, flex, stretch, or hold up their wrists, hands, arms, or shoulders.

▼ Using hand tools that have sharp edges or ridges, vibrate, exhaust air onto the hand, make excessive noise, are hard to hold or reach, do not operate smoothly, or have a grip span (the space between thumb and forefinger) of more than 4 inches

▼ Sitting, standing, leaning forward (particularly with the neck bent at more than 15 degrees), working in an immobile position, or performing static muscular work for long stretches of time

▼ Requiring excessive movements (lifting overhead, stretching, twisting, pushing, pulling, etc.)

▼ Awkward design of work components (work sites that don't work for particularly short or tall employees, work surfaces and chairs that don't adjust, inadequate visibility or lighting, necessary materials stored above the shoulder or below the knee, materials or tools that are hard to reach, inconvenient control panels, obstructed or slippery walkways, etc.)

▼ Work components that require unusual abilities (controls that require unusual force to operate, tasks that require workers' eyes to focus over various distances, extreme or frequent lifting requirements, moving large and clumsy units, etc.)

Self-Inspection Checklists are contained in Resources and Checklists Section H. They can help you develop a vigilant and safety-conscious crew.

MONEY SAVERS

⬇ Keep Information Readily Available

People in emergency situations often forget what they need to do. Back them up by putting information where they will need or use it. For example, the following information should be posted by every telephone:

- ▼ Company name (e.g., the name paramedics will see on the sign out front)
- ▼ Company address and cross street
- ▼ Company telephone number
- ▼ Emergency response numbers (police, fire, ambulance, hazardous response team, etc.)
- ▼ Information relative to hazardous substances

⬇ Know What to Avoid

Make sure that employees recognize and reduce the major causes of on-the-job accidents:

- ▾ Poor housekeeping
- ▾ Improper use of tools, equipment, and facilities
- ▾ Unsafe or defective equipment and facilities
- ▾ Lack of proper procedures
- ▾ Unsafe improvised procedures
- ▾ Failure to follow prescribed procedures
- ▾ Job not understood
- ▾ Lack of awareness of hazards involved
- ▾ Lack of proper tools, equipment, and facilities
- ▾ Lack of guards and safety devices
- ▾ Lack of protective clothing and equipment
- ▾ Exceeding prescribed limits (on load, speed, strength, etc.)
- ▾ Inattention to and neglect of safe practices
- ▾ Fatigue and reduced alertness
- ▾ Misconduct and poor attitude[1]

⬇ Institute Required OSHA Action Plans

Avoid costly fines by determining if your facility is required to have an emergency action plan. These plans are required for facilities covered by the following OSHA Act regulations:

- ▾ Powered Platforms for Building Maintenance
- ▾ Process Safety Management of Highly Hazardous Chemicals
- ▾ Hazardous Waste Operations and Emergency Response (HAZWOPER)
- ▾ Portable Fire Suppression Equipment
- ▾ Fixed Extinguishing Systems
- ▾ Fire Detection Systems

[1]Ted Ferry, *Modern Accident Investigation and Analysis,* 2nd ed. (New York: Wiley, 1988). Copyright © 1988. Reprinted by permission of John Wiley & Sons, Inc.

- ▼ Grain Handling Facilities
- ▼ Vinyl Chloride
- ▼ Cadmium
- ▼ DBPC
- ▼ Acrylonitrile
- ▼ Ethylene Oxide
- ▼ Methylenedianiline

At a minimum, these plans must include:

- ▼ Emergency escape procedures
- ▼ Emergency escape route assignments
- ▼ Procedures for employees who will evacuate after performing critical safety functions
- ▼ Procedures for determining if all employees have been evacuated
- ▼ Rescue duties
- ▼ Medical duties
- ▼ Procedures for reporting related emergencies (fires, immediate medical needs, etc.)
- ▼ Names or titles of people who can provide additional plan information or clarification

---

DURING THE ACCIDENT

Most carriers and companies have similar procedures for handling on-the-job accidents. These procedures cover three major areas: initial response, investigation and documentation, and formal reporting.

Initial Response

The company's initial response is necessarily a function of two things: becoming aware of the accident or injury and determining the victim's medical needs. Immediate awareness of the injury is crucial because it affects all that follows.

The bottom line is that *employees must inform their supervisors immediately when they or someone else is injured on the job.* The supervisor needs to be aware of even minor injuries (say, those requiring nothing more than an adhesive bandage or ice pack). Accidents can escalate or be initially misdiagnosed (e.g., an aspirin doesn't fix a concussion). *Note:* To minimize fraud, significant off-the-job injuries should also be reported to supervisors.

Immediate action must be taken once an authorized representative (line supervisor, staff manager, employer, etc.) has knowledge of the accident. Certain deadlines may also be legally imposed once this knowledge exists. Legally, knowledge of the accident exists if the representative:

- Sees the accident.
- Knows that a worker has been injured.
- Is informed verbally or in writing that an accident has occurred.
- Learns that a worker is going to file a claim relative to a condition that the company had not considered work related.
- Learns that a worker (or his representative) has directly approached the workers' compensation carrier.

Note: Depending on the severity of the injury, the supervisor may need to inform OSHA, the company's compensation carrier, or top management as soon as he becomes aware of the accident.

All victims must receive prompt and appropriate medical attention. A timely drug and alcohol test should be given to all appropriate individuals (e.g., any personnel who were involved in or contributed to the accident). The company should develop guidelines for supervisors indicating what type of medical treatment to provide or obtain for different types of injuries. A good rule of thumb is that the company can administer reasonable and prudent first aid; anything else must come from appropriate health care professionals. *Note:* As a corollary, if first aid is all that a victim requires, no workers' compensation report needs to be filed.

The guidelines must address the hazards common to your

facility, industry, and employees and pass both commonsense and legal tests, a condition that may be rather difficult to meet. For example, an employee of one of the authors, a gardener, was allergic to bee stings—so allergic that if he received multiple stings, he could go into anaphylactic shock in less than a minute. The problem? If he went into shock before he could inject an antidote, he would be unable to administer the medication himself and would probably die. Legally, his supervisor could not administer (or even provide) this emergency medication; he could not even discuss the employee's medical condition. Providing or administering the medication would be outside the parameters of giving first aid; discussing the employee's specific medical problem would be in violation of medical privacy.

The author did not want to break the law or put the employee in jeopardy, so he eventually discussed the general topic of first aid with employees at a safety meeting. He stated, as an example, that managers could not administer medications (adrenalin for bee stings, insulin to diabetics, etc.) even under emergency conditions. He also stated for the record that legally, under certain conditions, employees could. He suggested that if employees had a serious medical condition that could require emergency medication, they might consider voluntarily and publicly (e.g., for the record) acknowledging their condition to their peers, publicly (again for the record) asking their peers to administer the medication under certain well-defined medical conditions, and showing their peers where they kept their emergency medication and how to administer it.

In this instance, the gardener publicly discussed his condition with his peers and publicly asked for their assistance in the event of an emergency. They volunteered to help, and the grateful employee showed them what they needed to do should he receive multiple bee stings.

Investigation and Documentation

It is the supervisor's job to immediately protect, gather, and record information relative to any on-the-job accident. Because physical evidence, memories, and opinions change (and almost always for the worse) over time, the incident must be investigated and documented as quickly as possible.

In the event of an accident, the supervisor should:

1. *Note the time. In writing.*

2. Depending on the nature of the injury, *summon or give medical assistance.*

3. From the first moment of the accident, *express concern for the injured worker.* True concern diminishes the likelihood that the worker will file a false or exaggerated claim. Of course, sincere concern *must* be followed by sincere actions.

4. *Immediately order other employees to clear the area.* It is important that employees not inadvertently (or advertently) destroy, remove, replace, move, fix, alter, or use anything that could shed light on the incident. Employees can be told to leave the area to avoid personal trauma and protect their own physical safety.

5. *Identify and secure all of the witnesses. Note:* There are four categories of witnesses:

> (1) People who actually saw or were involved in the accident. Physical presence at the time and scene of the accident does not guarantee that a person belongs in this witness category.
> (2) People who came on the scene or otherwise became aware of the accident after it occurred.
> (3) People who saw the circumstances or events that led to the accident.
> (4) People who have background information regarding the victim's work habits, equipment involved, or anything else pertinent.

6. *Ask witnesses in the first three groups to identify themselves* by a show of hands. Each of these witnesses should be sent to a different, predetermined location. They should have no additional contact with other witnesses until they have been formally interviewed. *Note:* Interviews should be conducted as soon as possible, and employees or other witnesses must not leave work before they are interviewed. Over time, they are likely to forget (or misremember) crucial information. Witnesses in the first cat-

egory should be interviewed first, those in the second category should be interviewed next, and so on. Objective observations tend to fade over time, while opinions and conclusions increase. That's why you collect the most crucial information first.

7. Gather time-crucial physical data. Supervisors should always have access to a camera (with film), a measuring tape, and color swatches. Within a few minutes of the accident, they should take pictures of the injury, measure any bruised or swollen areas, and compare any bruises to the color swatches. Record all observations. This kind of documentation can be very helpful if fraud is detected or suspected. It helps answer the $64,000 question: Is the physical appearance of the injury (bruise color, swelling, etc.) consistent with the elapsed time? Could the injury have taken place earlier, say off the job?

8. *Have the safety manager secure the area physically.* Lock off entrances, post signs, cordon off hallways, and close windows. All physical evidence must be preserved until it can be seen and analyzed. *Note:* Once the victims have been rescued, OSHA inspectors may prohibit unauthorized access to the area. This is often the case when an accident involves a fatality, or the hospitalization of multiple workers. Check local regulations.

9. *Interview the witnesses.* The interviewer should try to keep the employee comfortable and let the employee know that he is required to provide honest and accurate information. It can be difficult to do these things simultaneously. If necessary, the latter need should take precedence over the former.

Inform the witness that the interview is going to be taped, transcribed, notarized, and submitted to him for his signature because anything he says can have legal repercussions—particularly (say this with a smile) if there is any hint of fraud. Letting an employee know that his interview is serious business, worth notarizing, makes it less likely that he will indulge in fraud, collusion, self-aggrandizing, tall tales, or speculation.

Conduct the interview in an informal setting. Let the employee tell the story in his own time and own way; don't ask questions or seek clarification until he has finished. Keep the tone friendly and the questions open-ended. Stress that the company isn't looking to place blame or identify a scapegoat; your objective is to identify the causes of the accident and eliminate them. Encourage the employee to provide details and to steer clear of conclusions.

10. *Gather general documentation.* Talk to others who can provide background information—for example: Is the equipment in good working order? Was it being used properly? Had there been prior problems with this employee or this machinery? Check the job site and equipment involved in the accident. Does it suggest anything? It is not uncommon for workers to tamper with things in an attempt to "create an accident." For example, if a worker slips on a wet floor and is injured, ask why water would be in that particular place at that particular time. Is there a reasonable source for the water (a window, roof leak, water fountain, etc.)? Had other workers been in the area? Had they noticed a puddle or walked through it, leaving wet footprints?

11. *Look for physical evidence of the accident itself*—for example: Is the amount of blood on the job site consistent with an immediate injury, or is it possible that a scab was torn off a weekend sports injury? Is the placement or pattern of blood believable?

Formal Reporting

Formal reporting is done at three levels. Any accident or near-miss incident should be reported, giving company personnel a chance to analyze and improve the conditions that precipitated it. If an accident is reportable, the supervisor (or other assigned party) needs to contact the workers' compensation carrier and submit the appropriate claim forms. If the accident meets certain criteria, you may also be required to report it to OSHA.

Before submitting a report to the workers' compensation carrier, determine if the accident is in fact reportable.

When to Report an Incident
- ▾ There was a fatality.
- ▾ The injured worker lost one or more workdays.
- ▾ The victim's employment was terminated.
- ▾ The injury required more than simple first aid.

▼ The victim lost consciousness, his range of motion, and/
   or the ability to perform his job.
▼ The employer has been informed that an employee has a
   diagnosed occupational illness.

If a report or claim is in order, the supervisor (or other assigned party) should prepare and submit it to the carrier as soon
as possible. Ideally, it should be reviewed by another party.

If the supervisor thinks fraud may be involved, he should
inform the workers' compensation carrier immediately and in-
formally: in a one-on-one meeting, a phone call, a note clipped
to the claim (not stapled—then it becomes a part of the formal
paperwork and can be subpoenaed). For legal purposes, the
company may choose to have someone other than the supervisor
(someone the employee would not readily suspect and thus
identify) report any suspicious findings.

As indicated earlier, certain injuries (such as fatalities, multiple employees requiring hospitalization, etc.) must be reported
to OSHA.

MONEY SAVERS

⬇ Provide Appropriate Medical Care

If the accident victim does not need immediate medical attention, the supervisor can call medical experts to see what kind
of attention the employee needs. Why visit an expensive emergency room when a doctor's office or simple clinic would suf-
fice?

⬇ Promote Early Accident Reports

Tell employees that waiting to report an on-the-job accident
makes the related claim appear suspect to your workers' compensation carrier. The benefit for you is that the sooner an
accident is reported, the less time and money it will take to
resolve.

There are eight major reasons that employees do not report accidents:

▼ Fear of discipline
▼ Concern about the record
▼ Concern for reputation
▼ Desire to prevent work interruption
▼ Desire to keep a personal record clear
▼ Avoidance of red tape
▼ Concern about attitudes of others
▼ Poor understanding of the accident's importance

Make sure that these justifications do not apply to your employees. For example, make it clear to employees that they will not be disciplined, criticized, or mocked for reporting accidents or having them on the record. Stress that reputation, work records, work interruptions, and red tape are less important than the employees' well-being. You want—you *need*—to know when employees are hurt or involved in a near miss.

⬇ Protect Evidence

Don't let concerned salespeople replace any tools or equipment that has been involved in an accident. They may not be trying to "get you back on your feet"; they may be trying to remove or destroy their faulty product.

AFTER THE ACCIDENT

After an accident, it is important to mitigate damages to both the company and the injured worker. The company is served by identifying the root causes of the accident and removing them; the worker is best served by an early return to work or a light-duty program.

Helping the Company

With help from employees, try to determine the root causes of the accident, and remove or minimize them. Then report any findings to top management and others in the company who could benefit.

Ideally, your company does the same things before an accident that it does after. You should educate all employees relative to safety and workers' compensation issues, in addition to looking for ways to improve site safety.

Try to combine the traditional before-an-accident attitude—pragmatic program planning and administration—with the typical after-an-accident attitude—shocked attention and concern. That's the best way to avoid during-the-accident dramas.

That said, after an accident, the supervisor or safety officer must identify all direct and indirect causes of the incident. A checklist of direct and indirect causes is contained in Resources and Checklists Section I.

Helping the Injured Employee Return to Work

Light duty is a means of bringing an injured employee back to work before he can physically resume his regular job. Light-duty programs help injured employees psychologically by getting them back on their feet; they help employers by minimizing workers' compensation costs and claims.

Under a light-duty program, employees with temporary partial disabilities are assigned physically appropriate tasks until they can return to their regular positions. From an employer's perspective, there are four forms of "light duty":

1. *Informal light duty with no medical involvement.* Say that Chris tells his supervisor that he strained his back playing softball. Chris's supervisor takes him off the assembly line and has him take inventory for the day. Chris gives his back a break.

This kind of light duty involves no legalities, no formal reports, and no record keeping. Legally, it is not light duty at all, simply a function of corporate common sense. It is in the supervisor's best interests, however, to note his action in a personal log.

2. *Informal light duty with no medical restrictions.* Lynn strains her back on the job and visits the physician, who reports the injury as a minor back sprain and releases Lynn back to work without any work restrictions. Still, her supervisor decides to play it safe and have Lynn run inventory numbers for a few days.

A workers' compensation report is filed, and a medical claim is made. Since there are no work restrictions or time loss, any peremptory changes made in the employee's temporary duties are not legally defined as light duty. Legally, Lynn is not defined as disabled. There should be little or no effect on your compensation policy.

Note: Your company can avoid any impact on its workers' compensation premium by paying the initial doctor's fee out of pocket, when and where legal. A report nevertheless will still need to be filed.

3. *Formal light duty with medical restrictions.* Jim strains his back on the job and visits a physician. The physician tells Jim that he can return to work but for the next two weeks is not to lift anything weighing more than 25 pounds. He does not have to return to the physician unless there are additional problems.

For courtesy and morale purposes, Jim should probably be placed at a job inside the plant that does not require a change in pay, position, or title. If he is a union member, he is probably guaranteed a similar pay level, position, and title. In either case, Jim's temporary duties and restrictions are communicated to him in writing. He (and, if relevant, his union) must accept and initial off on the temporary duty list.

This injury would be reported to the workers' compensation carrier as a lower back strain. Again, no claim or time loss is involved. Your compensation premium is only marginally affected. Jim is not legally defined as disabled.

4. *Formal light duty with time loss, temporary partial disability, and medical restrictions.* BT injures his back on the job and is off work for a week. In BT's state, a time-loss injury is one that re-

quires the worker to miss two or more days of work. A time-loss incident legally defines an injured employee as temporary partially disabled. A workers' compensation report and claim are filed; the carrier may eventually assign a claim reserve. BT cannot return to work in any capacity without his physician's approval. The physician's orders supersede those of his employer or the carrier.

The physician must develop a list of the duties and physical tasks that BT can perform. The physician can start from scratch or use a comprehensive job description and ability checklist provided by the employer. The second option is preferable.

BT's physician must evaluate and approve every component of his proposed light duty. What are BT's abilities relative to lifting, moving, standing, walking, bending, and squatting? Can he stand on the job? If the answer is yes, how long can he stand? Four hours a day? A whole day? With what kinds of breaks or physical supports?

There are four major benefits to a formal light duty policy. The first is *increased morale.* Employees appreciate employers who are willing to go the extra mile. Keeping an injured employee working, even under the toughest light duty restrictions, facilitates his eventual reintegration into the workplace. It also demonstrates to other employees that company loyalty works both ways: from the employee and toward the employee.

The second reason to utilize a formal light duty program is for *control purposes.* Having the injured employee at the workplace allows you to monitor his medical condition without appearing patriarchal or suspicious. As noted earlier, a good light duty program eliminates a major source of fraud.

The third reason for a formal light duty program is that it *speeds the employee's return to his regular duties.* Most employees miss the camaraderie of their peers and begin pushing for regular duty. People who have totally changed their lives and schedules are much more difficult to entice back to the work site.

Finally, a formal light duty program can *reduce workers' compensation costs.* Keeping an injured worker on the payroll means there are no heavy time-loss charges to drive up the premium.

MONEY SAVERS

⬇ Go to the Doctor's Office

One of the best ways to avoid fraud is a policy of accompany-
ing injured employees to the doctor. Stress to the physician
that the employee is wanted and needed; he is valued, and
you will do whatever is necessary to see that your light duty
offer meets his physical needs. Sit down with the physician
and the employee, and make sure that all parties agree on the
appropriateness of the temporary assignment.

This demonstration of active concern accomplishes two
things. First, it demonstrates to the physician that you re-
spect, and will abide by, his medical judgment. Physicians are
more likely to prescribe light duty for injured workers when
they know that the workers will receive appropriate support
from the employer. Second, workers are less likely to exaggerate their suffering or injuries when both employer and physician are present. The more information the parties share, the
more appropriate the doctor's medical restrictions will be.

Attitude is everything. Explain to the employee that with
his permission you would like to attend his medical appointments because you want to make sure you understand what
the company needs to do for him. If he expresses any reserva-
tions regarding your presence, drop the whole idea. Your goal
is to help, not hassle, the employee.

⬇ Implement a Light Duty Program

A light duty program is a bargain, especially if the government picks up a big chunk of the tab. Many states subsidize
light duty employment. The employee receives his normal,
preaccident income, the employer pays as little as 20 percent
of his wages, and the state government (usually through the
auspices of the unemployment department) picks up the rest.
Check with your state OSHA office for applicable incentives.

6

Reducing Workers' Compensation Fraud

Our fraud-riddled workers' compensation system is a working example of Schopenhauer's law of entropy:

> If you put a spoonful of wine in a barrel full of sewage, you get sewage.

> If you put a spoonful of sewage in a barrel full of wine, you get sewage.

In other words, it takes only one fraudulent claim to financially and psychologically damage your otherwise perfect program. The best way to minimize fraudulent claims is to take preventive action. Creating a misuser-unfriendly, antifraud environment takes work, but it can be a highly profitable undertaking.

HIRING CONSIDERATIONS

Almost anything is easier to get into than to get out of. That's why it's important, when interviewing and hiring personnel, to screen out fraud-oriented applicants. This means creating hiring policies and procedures that will help you identify and evade problematic people. Bottom line, *never* hire without conducting due diligence.

Job References

Checking job references thoroughly (and creatively) is one way to avoid fraud-oriented people or an actual fraud plan in progress. Both business and personal references can provide valuable insight into a worker's character.

The reference checks you make on potential employees should be at least as thorough as the ones you make on credit applicants. In fact, many of the techniques used to investigate credit applicants are appropriate for job applicants. Consider the following techniques and background information:

How to Check Applicants' References

1. Check the party giving the reference. Does the address given really exist? Does the business really exist?
2. Ask the business reference to send you a business card. If he can't get you one, you're not dealing with a real business.
3. Ask to talk to a second person at the reference business.
4. Refuse to accept telephone-only references.
5. Watch for references that come with no telephone number.
6. Watch any reference names that were given by previous frauds.
7. Refuse references that use known mail-drop addresses or zip codes.
8. Watch for addresses or telephone numbers that are listed for several reference sources. More than likely the references are friends or family members rather than business references.
9. Verify, using a telephone book or operator, the reference's telephone number and address.
10. Write off any business reference that answers the telephone with an unprofessional greeting like "Hello."
11. If your call is answered with a telephone number, make

sure you're not talking to an answering service; it could be employed by your applicant.

12. Beware when business phones are disconnected without any referral number.
13. Do not accept hand-delivered references.
14. Try to determine if the reference has anything direct to gain from your hiring decision.
15. If the reference person is a woman, get her full (e.g., maiden) name. Does it match the applicant's?[1]

You need to ask references the questions that will help you determine if the applicant had any short-term jobs that he didn't list on his application form or if he "somehow obtained finances/payments sufficient to survive without actively working." A good reference will be able to answer the following questions:

- ▼ How many times have you been asked to provide a reference for this person?
- ▼ How many times have you provided a reference?
- ▼ How many reference requests were within the last year?
- ▼ How many reference requests were made within the past three months?
- ▼ Who asked for the references, and when?
- ▼ What was the date of the most recent request?
- ▼ Where can I go for additional information on this person?

Of course, these questions are asked in addition to the more standard questions.

Potential references have far less interest in providing information than you have in receiving it. What is critical information to you is unappreciated and uncompensated extra work to them. To head off this problem, call potential references before mailing your request for information to tell them that it's coming. Include a reference release form to minimize any legal concerns. Use professional-quality reference forms (if the form doesn't

1. Lynn Tylczak, *The Prentice Hall Credit and Collection Answer Book* (Englewood Cliffs, N.J.: Prentice Hall, 1993).

look as if it is important to you, the references won't think it is either).

The Job Application Form

Knowledge is power. The more you know about an applicant (or employee), the better you can evaluate the facts surrounding a potential fraud. The more a con man knows about your anti-fraud policies, the less likely he is to pursue employment with your firm.

You can use your application form to discourage frauds from joining your firm and collect information that may help you in future fraud investigations. *Note:* Collect all of the relevant information you can up front. That's when people are the most lax about giving it.

You want to know:

▼ *The applicant's doctor of record.* Does the physician have a reputation for involvement in questionable workers' compensation claims? *Note:* Is this the doctor the employee eventually visits when and if he is hurt on the job? If not, why not?

▼ *If the applicant has out-of-state plates.* If so, does he include out-of-state employment on his application form? Has he been convicted of any relevant crimes in the other states?

▼ *The applicant's hobbies or sports.* Pay special attention to activities that could generate accidents or injuries similar to those that might occur on the job site. If the employee suffers a disabling injury, you can also investigate to see if he is inexplicably able to pursue his hobbies or sports. The television program *Inside Edition* reported that in Michigan, a woman recently lost her workers' compensation disability income when her ex-husband sent the state attorney general a video of her participating in a "coleslaw wrestling tournament." (She was wrestling, with a bikini on, in a child's swimming pool full of coleslaw. Really!) Her attorney argued that since she did not win the tournament, she was in fact disabled. He lost the case.

▼ *Whether the applicant earns any extra income with other job skills (repair or carpentry work, landscaping, sewing, etc.), particu-*

larly job skills that are often purchased on a cash basis. An applicant may obtain employment with your company with the intent of "suffering a long-term, disabling injury" and then supplementing his ensuing disability income with underground economy employment.

Consider this story:

Last year Daniel Kriek [the names have been changed to protect the gullible] hired the "sweetest little old lady you'd ever want to meet." This year he wishes he never had. The founder of seven-year-old apparel maker Alpha Blouse Corp (ABC) met the woman when she called on ABC for a job "at any wage, just to finish out my time." Kriek put her to work cleaning desks, hardly suspecting that the time she had in mind was exactly ten working days. Employed on June 1, 1993, she requested a furlough on June 15. "You just started!" Kriek thought but didn't have the heart to utter. "When you're ready to come back," he said instead, "give us a call."

The woman never phoned. But her lawyer did. His little old client was filing a claim against ABC, the solicitor informed Kriek, because she had gotten double carpal tunnel syndrome, a job-related debilitation that prevented her from performing work of any kind. But not to fret: generous severance pay would be recompense enough for her to drop the claim. "How can you get carpal tunnel from 10 days behind a duster, even if you swing the feathers wrong?" Kriek demanded. The answer came months and "lots of legal fees" later, when the case, contested to the end by the incensed founder, was settled on the courthouse steps. "She knew what she was doing, big-time," an embittered Kriek concludes. "She was going for $20,000 per wrist." His investigation revealed that she'd engaged the lawyer before applying to ABC.[2]

2. Robert A. Mamis, "Employees from Hell," *Inc.* (January 1995).

You want the applicant to know:

▼ The legal ramifications of attempting (or in any way facilitating) a fraudulent workers' compensation claim. State on your application form that anyone filing a false claim or exaggerating a legitimate one will be prosecuted to the fullest extent of the law. Also state that any witness who provides false information will be prosecuted or terminated, or both.

▼ As a condition of employment (or continuing employment) an injured worker is required to accept a medically appropriate light-duty assignment. Most frauds, who want to take the money and run, will not run the risk of working for you!

MONEY SAVERS

⬇ **Second-Guess Applicants**

Try to determine the motives behind the applicant's interest in your company (and your motives for possibly hiring him). If he doesn't have a good or reasonable explanation for coming to see you, perhaps you'd better look a little further.

⬇ **Use Information From Other Sources**

Local information cooperatives can be an inexpensive and helpful source of applicant research. Employers can inform others when they have an employee (who must remain nameless!) leave immediately after filing a workers' compensation claim or receiving a settlement. Businesses who are advertising or looking for new employees can do what they want with the knowledge.

CREATING AN ANTIFRAUD WORK ENVIRONMENT

It's important for a business to build the right organizational attitude. The company mantra should be, "All for one and one for all" rather than, "All for one and that one is *me!*" A company with team spirit is a company with less workers' compensation fraud.

Educating the Workforce

Employees usually don't know very much about workers' compensation. They typically know even less about fraud within the system and why it is a problem—or, rather, why it is *their* problem. Education creates awareness. Once employees are aware of what workers' compensation costs the company (and costs them personally), they are less likely to submit, condone, or facilitate (via false witness) a fraudulent claim.

Employees need reality checks as much as they need paychecks. They should be told (and continuously reminded) that:

▼ *Workers' compensation fraud costs our economy millions of dollars every year.* That's money you and other employers can't use for raises, bonuses, promotions, additional staff, profit sharing, retirement contributions, better health care benefits, additional vacation or sick leave, on-site child care, improved working conditions, employee education or training, or business growth.

▼ *It is hard to perpetuate a fraud.* A fraud has to fake his injury twenty-four hours a day or risk being found out by a fraud investigator, reward-seeking friend, or coworker. Just what is it worth to be forced to spend twenty-four hours a day in a wheelchair or in braces or on one's back in a hospital bed?

Good health is a priceless thing. So is the opportunity to enjoy it. It's not worth compromising for a few bucks. *Note:* Because time loss is usually not 100 percent reimbursed and light duty assignments often pay less than regular duty, a fraudulent claim may cause the employee to lose money.

▼ *Fraud creates an atmosphere of distrust.* Consider the following:

Have you ever seen a maximum security prison? It's not a pretty sight. Here's what you'd see:

▾ Lots of guards watching the prisoners' every move
▾ Security cameras
▾ Strip searches
▾ Limited access
▾ A siege mentality

Have you ever seen a business with a high rate of internal theft or fraud? Here's what you'd see:

▾ Lots of guards watching the prisoners' every move
▾ Security cameras
▾ Personal searches
▾ Limited access
▾ A siege mentality

Prisons and businesses plagued by theft (or fraud) have strong parallels. If you want to work in a prison, become a corrections officer. If you don't, help the company prevent fraud. Don't let bad apples pollute your work environment.[3]

Workers' compensation fraud makes things harder on honest workers. Those who participate, condone, or facilitate fraudulent claims risk losing their jobs, livelihood, reputations, self-respect, references, and sometimes their freedom. Clearly, such fraud carries a high price tag for both victims and perpetrators.

Developing Antifraud Attitudes

The best way to take a bite out of workers' compensation crime is to help honest employees sink their teeth into the problem. By creating an atmosphere in which fraud is unacceptable, your workers can be your first line of defense against workers' compensation fraud.

To create an antifraud environment, you must be direct about fraud and its implications. For example, avoid euphemisms. Workers' compensation fraud is stealing—a serious crime that is punishable by incarceration. Use ugly words for an

---

3. Thomas E. Sheets, ''Preventing Workplace Theft'' (Menlo Park, Calif.: Crisp Publications, 1992). Reprinted with permission. Crisp Publications, Inc., 1200 Hamilton Court, Menlo Park, CA 94025. 800-442-7477 or 415-323-6100.

ugly concept. Also use posters or other indirect media to ask your employees thought-provoking, rhetorical questions—for example:

- ▼ What would your parents, spouse, or children say if they knew you were a criminal?
- ▼ Would you do this in the open? If you have to be ashamed of or secretive about what you do, how can you have any self-respect?
- ▼ How would you feel about someone else (a workers' compensation con man) getting the same paycheck without doing any work? Is that fair to you?

MONEY SAVERS

⬇ Institute Employee Incentives

Employees who report suspicious accidents or claims to their supervisors should receive financial rewards. Thus, there is an incentive for protecting—rather than cheating—the system.

⬇ Get Help From the Union

Because an antifraud environment benefits employees, it also benefits their union. Enlist the union's help in minimizing illegitimate workers' compensation claims. *Note:* The union can even help fraudulent followers by reminding them what they stand to lose if their duplicity is recognized and punished.

⬇ Enlist Your Compensation Carrier's Help

Compensation carriers can be used to create an antifraud environment. Seminars that cover fraud (how to detect it, what it costs the company and its employees, the criminal penalties, etc.) can generate awareness and cause potential frauds to rethink their positions.

ACCIDENTS: BEFORE AND AFTER

Ideally, accident documentation occurs both before and after an accident. Documenting before an accident or claim creates a baseline for comparison; documenting after an accident or claim allows you to identify suspicious changes, behaviors, or situations.

Before an Accident

Start documenting accidents today (as they say, any task worth doing was worth doing yesterday). Don't wait for an accident to occur (or seem to occur). Actions you take every day can make it difficult for an employee to claim that an off-the-job injury occurred on the job.

The employees think you're being friendly. You're actually being smart—very smart. You make sure that:

1. Every morning you or other management or supervisory personnel can greet workers before they enter the building. Keep your smile large and your eyes open. Are any workers limping? Favoring a leg or arm? Opening the door with their left (rather than their right) hand? Walking more slowly than usual? Shielding parts of their body (wearing sunglasses, wearing a long-sleeved coat on a hot day, etc.)?

2. Workers do warm-up exercises to get themselves physically prepared for a hectic day. Again, smile (or participate) and watch. Are any workers having a hard time keeping up? Does their mobility (as they raise legs, stretch, bend, or twist) seem impaired? Are they unable to do specific exercises (say, unable to do push-ups because of an injured hand) or balance themselves properly?

3. You casually ask employees every Friday afternoon what they have planned for the weekend. Beware of the employee who plans to ski on Sunday and then—surprise!—happens to sprain his ankle the first thing Monday morning. On company time, of course.

4. Ask all employees when they sign out to initial off on a "no accidents this week" report. Remind them that for their own protection and ease of claim investigation and documentation, accidents must be reported immediately. This helps avoid the "I didn't remember to report my Friday afternoon accident until Monday morning" syndrome.

5. Outside security cameras (and perhaps even inside security cameras) are used to "ensure employee safety." Keep the outside tapes on file for at least a week. They document employee behavior. If anything changes the day of an accident (e.g., the employee came in a new door, entered in a physically new or unusual way, arrived at a suspiciously early or late time, came via a new mode of transportation), it's usually a sign of fraud.

Any of these measures must be implemented in a positive approach. Security measures protect (as well as monitor) employees. Antifraud measures protect employees' (as well as the employer's) interests. A sincere interest in and awareness of employees generates goodwill as it mitigates fraud. Remember, you are not out to get employees; you are out to stop fraud!

After an Accident

Know what you're looking for. When a claim seems legitimate, document the accident. When it seems suspect, document the accident while looking for signs of fraud. They usually aren't hard to find.

Quickly and quietly inform your carrier when you think a worker is filing or is about to file a fraudulent claim. Your carrier has the experts necessary to document the supposed fraud; furthermore, if the claim later turns out to be legitimate, you haven't alienated yourself from the victim or his peers.

Red Flags for Fraud

▾ The employee reports an accident on Monday morning that he says occurred the prior Friday. Other delays should also be considered suspect.
▾ There were no witnesses to the accident.

▼ The employee just retained a new doctor or lawyer (ones known for questionable work on behalf of workers' compensation claimants).

▼ The victim has a history of filing previous workers' compensation claims or malingering on the job.

▼ Items such as tools or equipment that were involved in the accident did not belong at the job site.

▼ It appears that the workers has made a complete recovery (although he claims otherwise).

▼ The injured worker refuses a second medical opinion, reasonable diagnostic procedure (necessary to confirm his injury or condition), light duty assignment, or medical release for work.

▼ Coworkers indicate that the employee is actively engaged in sports, hobbies, or other work.

▼ The worker changes doctors frequently (particularly after they give him positive news).

▼ According to the rehabilitation report, the victim shows up muscular, tanned, and with calluses on his hands (or grease under his fingernails).

▼ The employee will release his post office box number but not the address of his actual residence.

▼ The worker's demands and disability are beyond what is typical for this kind of accident or injury.

▼ You are faced with dueling docs: One says the worker is well, and the other (e.g., the victim's physician) swears he is disabled.

▼ The worker recently took out a disability policy.

▼ You have a difficult time contacting the bedridden or otherwise disabled victim at home.

▼ There are significant differences between the employee's initial description of the accident and what can be documented through the medical examination or records.

▼ The accident occurred just before a job layoff, strike, termination, early retirement, or the end of a project or seasonal work.

▼ The victim has moved out of state.

▼ The employee saw a doctor just prior to the accident.

MONEY SAVERS

⬇ Give Frauds a Way Out

One way to ruffle an employee who is about to file a fraudulent workers' compensation claim is to ask him plainly if he is really sure he wants to file it. Give him pause to think. He's taking the first step in a long journey; if he's not careful, it could end in the penitentiary.

⬇ Maintain Good Records

Make sure that all of your records are orderly and up-to-date. What does that have to do with fraud? It's simple. Frauds want a payoff; they don't care if it comes from you or the state. If a fraudulent comp claim appears too dangerous, the con man may change his tack and threaten to "call in the dogs" (IRS, OSHA, EPA, FDA, state health board, etc.) and report or charge business irregularities unless you pay him off.

⬇ Don't Create Problems

Turn frauds over to your workers' compensation carrier immediately. You don't want to take any questionable actions that could make a bad situation worse. Remember that filing a fraudulent workers' compensation claim is a criminal act. Frauds are desperate people who will resort to desperate measures to get what they want. You have to think and act defensively. The fraud should be the one in trouble, not you. Consider this story:

> The management of a $5 million equipment repair service outside Philadelphia was criminally served by a piqued employee. The company had been patiently tolerating that worker's taking unannounced absences beyond the company's specified annual allotment. The worker's grounds were that his bursitis

flared up unpredictably and rendered his arm use-less. One day the company's operating officer happened by the worker's home and was astounded to see the absentee vigorously polishing his car with the supposedly incapacitated arm.

On the worker's return, the operating officer and a supervisor beckoned him into an office to discuss the inconsistency. So as not to disturb the clerks outside, they shut the door, whereupon the worker turned on his heels and departed. The next day a sheriff served each manager with criminal complaints. Among them were (as they were actually stated) interference with the exercise of civil rights, assault and battery, stalking and kidnapping. "I was held in a locked room against my will," the worker told the court. "Each time I tried to leave, the defendant threatened me. . . . The defendant pulled my arm so hard that he injured my shoulder permanently." A criminal trial was scheduled. While the plaintiff spent nothing, the defendants were obliged to pay for lawyers because directors' and officers' liability insurance doesn't cover criminal charges.[4]

⬇ Stay in Control

Losing your cool can be an expensive mistake. Need help keeping your temper? Remember that "employees from hell" are often employees who have been through hell. That's no excuse, but it does offer some perspective.

---

4. Mamis, "Employees From Hell."

Epilogue

You've probably noticed a common theme throughout this book: Trust everybody . . . but cut the cards. You can trust your workers' compensation carrier to offer you the coverage you need at an appropriate price. *But* you should ensure that your workers are assigned to the right job class (e.g., the lowest-cost job class that applies to their job and tasks). You should check claim reserves and argue against any that seem unnecessary. You should determine if your experience modifier truly reflects your safety track record. You should investigate any ballast figures or discounts that may apply to your firm.

You can trust OSHA to help you develop a safe and healthy job environment. *But* you should do what you can to avoid involuntary inspections. You should know how to handle involuntary inspections and request voluntary inspections in an attempt to limit involuntary inspections or fines. You should keep up to date with OSHA regulations, any required training, and your own paperwork.

You can trust your workers (or get rid of the ones you can't trust) to perform their duties in the safest manner possible. *But* you should continually check to make sure that employees wear the required personal protective equipment. You should repeat, repeat, repeat safety information until your memos and lectures sound like edicts from the Department of Redundancy Department. You should insist that employees sign off on training, safety, and personnel information. You should check out any suspicious accidents or claims.

And there you have the second theme: "You should." It all boils down to you. You should always keep a handle on your workers' compensation components. Good strategies and control will lead to a reduction in accidents, claims, and costs.

Resources and Checklists

A. State-by-State Safety and OSHA Sources

These are the state-by-state governmental sources for information about workers' compensation, OSHA, and OSHA-approved state safety systems.

Alabama: Commissioner, Department of Labor, 1789 Congressman Dickinson Dr., Montgomery, AL 36130. *Phone* (334) 242-3460; *fax* (334) 242-3417.

Alaska: Director, Division of Labor Standards and Safety, P.O. Box 107021, Anchorage, AK 99510. *Phone:* (907) 269-4914; *fax:* (907) 465-3584.

Arizona: Director, Industrial Commission, P.O. Box 19070, Phoenix, AZ 85005-9070. *Phone:* (602) 542-4411.

Arkansas: Director, Department of Labor, 10421 West Markham, Suite 100, Little Rock, AR 72205. *Phone:* (501) 682-4500; *fax:* (501) 682-4532.

California: Director, Department of Industrial Relations, 455 Golden Gate Ave., San Francisco, CA 94102. *Phone:* (415) 703-4590.

Colorado: Director, Risk Management Division, Department of

Administration, 225 East 16th St., 6th Fl., Denver, CO 80202. *Phone:* (303) 866-3848; *fax:* (303) 894-2409.

Connecticut: Director, Occupational Safety and Health, Department of Labor, 38 Wolcott Hill Rd., Wethersfield, CT 06109. *Phone:* (203) 566-4550.

Delaware: Director, Division of Industrial Affairs, Department of Labor, 820 North French St., Wilmington, DE 19801. *Phone:* (302) 577-2877; *fax:* (302) 577-3750.

Florida: Director, Division of Safety, Department of Labor and Employee Security, 2002 Old Saint Augustine Rd., Tallahassee, FL 32399-0663. *Phone:* (904) 488-3044.

Georgia: Deputy Commissioner, Department of Labor, 184 International Blvd., Suite 600, Atlanta, GA 30303. *Phone:* (404) 656-3028.

Hawaii: Administrator, Occupational Safety and Health Division, Department of Labor and Industrial Relations, 830 Punchbowl St., Room 423, Honolulu, HI 96813. *Phone:* (808) 586-9116.

Idaho: Director, Labor and Industrial Services, 277 North Sixth St., Boise, ID 83720. *Phone:* (208) 334-3950.

Illinois: Chairman, State Industrial Commission, 100 West Randolph St., Suite 8-272, Chicago, IL 60601. *Phone:* (312) 814-5559; *fax:* (312) 814-6523

Indiana: Deputy Commissioner, Occupational Safety and Health Administration, Department of Labor, AGC-South, Room W195, Indianapolis, IN 46204. *Phone:* (307) 232-3325.

Iowa: Administrator, Occupational Safety and Health, Department of Employment Services, 1000 East Grand, Des Moines, IA 50319. *Phone:* (515) 281-3606.

Kansas: Director, Division of Labor Management and Employment Standards, Department of Human Resources, 512 Southwest 6th Ave., Topeka, KS 66603-3174. *Phone:* (913) 296-7475; *fax:* (913) 296-1775.

Kentucky: Secretary, Labor Cabinet, 1049 U.S. 127 South Frankfort, KY 40601. *Phone:* (504) 342-7692.

Louisiana: Assistant Secretary, Department of Labor, P.O. Box 94094, Baton Rouge, LA 70804. *Phone:* (504) 342-7692.

Maine: Director, Bureau of Labor Standards, Department of

Labor, State House Station 45, Augusta, ME 04333. *Phone:* (207) 624-6400.

Maryland: Assistant Commissioner, Occupational Safety and Health, Department of Licensing and Regulations, 501 Saint Paul Pl., Baltimore, MD 21202-2272. *Phone:* (301) 333-4195.

Massachusetts: Director, Division of Industrial Safety, Department of Labor and Industries, 100 Cambridge St., Boston, MA 02202. *Phone:* (617) 727-3454.

Michigan: Director, Bureau of Safety and Regulation, Department of Labor, P.O. Box 30015, Lansing, MI 48909. *Phone:* (517) 322-1814.

Minnesota: OSHA Management Team, Department of Labor and Industry, 443 Lafayette Rd., Saint Paul, MN 55155. *Phone:* (612) 296-2116.

Mississippi: Director, Occupational Safety and Health, Workers' Compensation Commission, 2096 North State St., Suite 201, Jackson, MS 39216. *Phone:* (601) 987-3981.

Missouri: Director, Division of Labor Standards, Department of Labor and Industrial Relations, 3315 West Truman Blvd., Box 449, Jefferson City, MO 65102. *Phone:* (314) 751-3403; *fax:* (314) 751-3721.

Montana: Chief, Workers' Compensation Division, Department of Labor, 1805 Prospect, P.O. Box 8011, Helena, MT 59604-8011. *Phone:* (406) 444-6424.

Nebraska: Director, Labor and Safety Standards Division, Department of Labor, P.O. Box 94600, Lincoln, NE 68509. *Phone:* (402) 471-4712.

Nevada: Administrator, Occupational Safety and Health, Department of Industrial Relations, 1370 South Curry St., Carson City, NV 89710. *Phone:* (702) 687-5240; *fax:* (702) 687-6305.

New Hampshire: Commissioner, Department of Labor, 95 Pleasant St., Concord, NH 03301. *Phone:* (603) 271-3171.

New Jersey: Assistant Commissioner, Division of Workplace Standards, Department of Labor, John Fitch Plaza, CN 110, Trenton, NJ 08625. *Phone:* (609) 777-0249.

New Mexico: Bureau Chief, Occupational Health and Safety Bureau, Department of Health, 1190 Saint Francis, Box 26110, Santa Fe, NM 87502-0968. *Phone:* (505) 827-4230; *fax:* (505) 827-4422.

New York: Commissioner, Department of Labor, State Office Building, State Campus, Albany, NY 12240. *Phone:* (518) 457-2741.

North Carolina: Commissioner, Department of Labor, 4 West Edenton St., Raleigh, NC 27603. *Phone:* (919) 733-7166; *fax:* (919) 733-6197.

North Dakota: Director of Loss Prevention, Workers' Compensation Bureau, 500 East Front Ave., Bismarck, ND 58504-5685. *Phone:* (701) 328-3886; *fax:* (701) 328-3750.

Ohio: Superintendent, Division of Safety and Hygiene, Industrial Commission, 246 North High St., Columbus, OH 43266-0564. *Phone:* (614) 752-4463; *fax:* (614) 644-5707.

Oklahoma: Supervisor, Safety Standards Division, Department of Labor, 1315 Broadway Pl., Oklahoma City, OK 73105. *Phone:* (405) 523-1500.

Oregon: Administrator, Occupational Safety and Health Administration, 160 Labor Industries Building, 350 Winter St. NE, Salem, OR 97310. *Phone:* (503) 378-3272.

Pennsylvania: Director, Occupational and Industrial Safety, Department of Labor and Industry, 1529 Labor and Industry Building, Harrisburg, PA 17120. *Phone:* (717) 787-3323.

Rhode Island: Occupational Safety and Health, Department of Labor, 220 Elmwood Ave., Providence, RI 02907. *Phone:* (401) 457-1800.

South Carolina: Administrator, Occupational Safety and Health, Labor/Licensing/Regulations Department, P.O. Box 11329, Columbia, SC 29211. *Phone:* (803) 734-9644.

South Dakota: Director, Division of Labor and Management, Department of Labor, Kneip Building, Pierre, SD 57501. *Phone:* (605) 773-3101.

Tennessee: Director, Occupational Safety, Department of Labor, 501 Union Building, Nashville, TN 37243-0659. *Phone:* (615) 741-2793.

Texas: Commissioner, Department of Health, 1100 West 49th St., Austin, TX 78756. *Phone:* (512) 458-7111.

Utah: Administrator, Occupational Safety and Health Division, State Industrial Commission, 160 East 300 South, Salt Lake City, UT 84114. *Phone:* (801) 530-6898.

Vermont: Manager, Division of Occupational Safety and Health

Administration, Department of Labor and Industry, North Building, National Life, Montpelier, VT 05620. *Phone:* (802) 828-2765; *fax:* (802) 828-2748.

Virginia: Commissioner, Department of Labor and Industry, 13 South 13th St., Richmond, VA 23219. *Phone:* (804) 786-2377.

Washington: Assistant Director, Industrial Safety and Health, Department of Labor and Industries, P.O. Box 44700, Olympia, WA 98504-4600. *Phone:* (360) 902-5580.

West Virginia: Commissioner, Division of Labor, State Capitol Complex, Building 3, Charleston, WV 25305. *Phone:* (304) 558-7890.

Wisconsin: Administrator, Division of Safety and Buildings, Department of Industrial Labor and Human Relations, 201 East Washington, Room 103, P.O. Box 7969, Madison, WI 53705. *Phone:* (608) 266-3151; *fax:* (608) 267-9566.

Wyoming: Administrator, Division of Occupational Safety and Health Administration, Department of Employment, Herschler Building, Cheyenne, WY 82002. *Phone:* (307) 777-7700.

District of Columbia: Associate Director, Occupational Safety and Health Office, Department of Employment Services, 950 Upshur St., NW, Washington, DC, 20011. *Phone:* (202) 576-6339.

Guam: Director, Department of Labor, P.O. Box 9970, Tamuning, GU 96911. *Phone:* (671) 647-4142; *fax:* (671) 646-9004.

Northern Mariana Islands: Director, Department of Labor, P.O. Box 10007, Saipan, MP 96950. *Phone:* (670) 664-2000; *fax:* (670) 664-2020.

Puerto Rico: Secretary, Department of Labor and Human Resources, 505 Muñoz Rivera Ave., Hato Rey, PR 00918. *Phone:* (809) 754-5353.

U.S. Virgin Islands: Commissioner, Department of Labor, P.O. Box 208, St. Thomas, VI 00802. *Phone:* (809) 776-3700; *fax:* (809) 773-0094.

B. Sample Federal OSHA Regulation With Sample State System Amendments

Federal OSHA for Personal Protective Equipment (PPE)—Foot Protection

(a) General Requirements. Each affected employee shall wear protective footwear when working in areas where there is a danger of foot injuries due to falling and rolling objects, or objects piercing the sole, and where such employee's feet are exposed to electrical hazards.

(b) Criteria for protective footwear

    (1) Protective footwear purchased after July 5, 1994, shall comply with ANSI Z41-1991, "American National Standard for Personal Protection—Protective Footwear," which is incorporated by reference, or shall be demonstrated by the employer to be equally effective. This incorporation by reference was approved by the Director of the Federal Register in accordance with 5 U.S.C. 552(a) and 1 CFE part 51. Copies may be obtained from the American

National Standards Institute. Copies may be inspected at the Docket Office, Occupational Safety and Health Administration, U.S. Department of Labor, 200 Constitution Ave., NW, Room N2634, Washington, D.C., or at the Office of the Federal Register, 800 North Capitol Street NW, Suite 700, Washington, D.C.

(2) Protective footwear purchased before July 5, 1994, shall comply with the ANSI standard "USA Standard for Men's Safety-Toe Footwear," Z41.1-1967, which is incorporated by reference, or shall be demonstrated by the employer to be equally effective. This incorporation by reference was approved by the Director of the Federal Register in accordance with 5 U.S.C. 552(a) and 1 CFR part 51. Copies may be obtained from the American National Standards Institute. Copies may be inspected at the Docket Office, Occupational Safety and Health Administration, U.S. Department of Labor, 200 Constitution Ave., NW, Room N2634, Washington, D.C., or at the Office of the Federal Register, 800 North Capitol Street, NW, Suite 700, Washington, D.C.

State OSHA for Personal Protective Equipment (PPE)—Foot Protection

States with their own occupational safety and health programs often develop their regulations by augmenting or strengthening existing federal statutes. For example, Oregon adds these requirements to the federal OSHA Act standard:

(3) Special types or designs of shoes or foot guards are required where conditions exist that make their use necessary for the safety of workers.

(4) Leggings or high boots of leather, rubber or other suitable material shall be worn by persons exposed to hot substances or dangerous chemical spills.

C. Sample State Extraterritoriality Statute

Coverage while temporarily in or out of state; judicial notice of other states' laws; agreement between states relating to conflicts of jurisdiction; limitation on compensation for claims in this state and other jurisdictions.

(1) If a worker employed in this state and subject to this chapter temporarily leaves the state incidental to that employment and receives an accidental injury arising out of and in the course of employment, the worker, or beneficiaries of the worker if the injury results in death, is entitled to the benefits of this chapter as though the worker were injured within this state.

(2) Any worker from another state and the employer of the worker in that other state are exempted from the provisions of this chapter while the employer has a temporary workplace within this state and the worker is within this state doing work for the employer;

> (a) If that employer has furnished Workers' Compensation insurance coverage under the Workers' Compensation insurance or similar laws of a state other than this one so as to cover that worker's employment while in this state;

(b) If the extraterritorial provisions of this chapter are recognized in that other state; and

(c) If employers and workers who are covered in this state are likewise exempted from the application of the Workers' Compensation insurance or similar laws of the other state. The benefits under the Workers' Compensation Insurance Act or similar laws of the other state, or other remedies under a like Act or laws, are the exclusive remedy against the employer for any injury, whether resulting in death or not, received by the worker while working for that employer in this state.

(3) A certificate from the duly authorized officer of the department or similar department of another state certifying that the employer of the other state is insured therein and has provided extraterritorial coverage insuring workers while working within this state is prima facie evidence that the employer carries that Workers' Compensation insurance.

(4) Whenever in any appeal or other litigation the construction of the laws of another jurisdiction is required, the courts shall take judicial notice thereof.

(5) The Director of the Department of Consumer and Business Services shall have authority to enter into agreements with the Workers' Compensation agencies of other states relating to conflicts of jurisdiction where the contract of employment is in one state and the injuries are received in the other state, or where there is a dispute as to the boundaries or jurisdiction of the states and when such agreements have been executed and made public by the respective state agencies, the rights of workers hired in such other state and injured while temporarily in this state, or hired in this state and injured while temporarily in another state, or where the jurisdiction is otherwise uncertain, shall be determined pursuant to such agreement and confined to the jurisdiction provided in such agreements.

(6) When a worker has a claim under the Workers' Compensation law of another state, territory, province or foreign nation for the same injury or occupational disease as the claim filed in this state, the total amount of compensation paid or awarded

under such other Workers' Compensation law shall be credited against the compensation due under this state's Workers' Compensation law. The worker shall be entitled to the full amount of compensation due under this state's law. If this state's compensation is more than the compensation under another law, or compensation paid the worker under another law is recovered from the worker, the insurer shall pay any unpaid compensation to the worker up to the amount required by the claim under this state's law.

(7) For the purpose of this section, "temporary workplace" does not include a single location within this state where the employer's work is performed by one or more workers for more than 30 days in a calendar year.

D. OSHA Inspection Information

The following OSHA questions are taken from an actual OSHA investigation interview.

Questions Aimed at Supervisors

Safety Committee Questions

- Is there a written safety committee meeting agenda?
- Do you hold regular safety committee meetings?
- Are quarterly inspections being conducted?
- Are committee minutes being kept? Who keeps them? Where are they?
- Are reports, evaluations, and recommendations made by the committee part of the records?
- Does the employer respond in writing to safety committee recommendations?
- Is there a way for employees not on the safety committee to make suggestions?
- Are those employees' suggestions made part of the record?

The material in this section of Resources and Checklists comes from the Cascade Employers Association and is used with permission.

▾ Do you evaluate the company's accident and illness prevention program?

▾ Have you established procedures for workplace inspections?

▾ Are inspections conducted at least quarterly?

▾ Are recommendations made to the employer on how to eliminate the hazards?

▾ Are an employee and a management person on the inspection team? If so, who are they?

▾ Have these people on the team been trained on hazard inspection? If so, when?

▾ Does the committee do accident investigation?

▾ Has the committee been trained for investigations? When?

▾ Who is responsible for writing company safety policy?

▾ What duties and responsibilities has the company given the safety committee?

Training Questions

▾ What type of training does the company provide for supervisors and management?

▾ Who is responsible?

▾ Who receives it?

▾ When was the last time you received training?

▾ Who conducted it?

▾ When was the training conducted?

▾ Who do you think is accountable for training?

▾ Who evaluates training?

▾ How does the company know you are trained?

▾ What language is the training given in?

▾ Is the training oral or written in this company?

▾ How many languages do employees that you supervise speak?

▾ How many employees speak a different language?

▾ Does the company use an interpreter?

Safety Policy

▾ Have you ever seen this safety policy before?

▾ When did you last see it?

▾ Was it given to you orally, or was it written?

▾ How do you share it with the employees whom you supervised?

▾ Did you read the part about safety?

▾ Is it in some other languages?

▾ Have you ever enforced this policy? If so, when?

▾ Is there any written record of this disciplinary action?

▾ Has this policy ever been enforced to your knowledge? If so, when?

▾ Do you know if there is a written record of that action?

▾ Has a supervisor, a manager, or an owner ever talked to you about the policy?

▾ Have you ever had an employee sign something that said he or she read the policy?

▾ According to the policy you should not work on a machine without being trained. Are you trained?

▾ Were you trained, and do you feel that it was adequate? Explain.

▾ Do you feel you were trained well enough to supervise your employees?

▾ How do you evaluate the training of your employees?

Lockout and Tagout

▾ What action was taken before going into machinery with moving parts?

▾ Was there a lockout/tagout program? Before the accident? After the accident?

▾ Did management know about the program?

▾ Who do you think should have been responsible for the lockout/tagout?

▾ Did management ask the employees using the machine the best way to guard it?

▾ How often does someone go into danger areas?

▾ Did you ever see the person in the danger area?

▾ Did you know the person went into the danger area while the machine was still running?

▾ Tell me about the supervisor and supervision within the company.

- ▼ In what level of supervision are you?
- ▼ Do you know who your supervisor is?
- ▼ Do you know who that person's supervisor is?
- ▼ Do you know who your supervisor's supervisor is?
- ▼ Do you know who the person is?
- ▼ Do you know who is responsible for training?
- ▼ What other responsibility does this or these people have?
- ▼ Have you ever received training from them before?

Questions Aimed at Employees

- ▼ What type of training does the company provide for supervisors and management?
- ▼ Who is responsible?
- ▼ Who receives it?
- ▼ When was the last time you received training?
- ▼ Who conducted it?
- ▼ Who do you think is accountable for training?
- ▼ Who evaluates training?
- ▼ How does the supervisor know you are trained?
- ▼ What languages is the training given in?
- ▼ How many employees speak both languages that the company uses?
- ▼ Who acts as an interpreter for the company?
- ▼ Is the safety training oral or written?
- ▼ Is it given in as many languages as all employees speak?
- ▼ Have you ever seen this safety policy before?
- ▼ Was it oral or written?
- ▼ Did you read the part about safety? Is it in other languages?
- ▼ Has it ever been enforced before?
- ▼ Has a supervisor talked to you about the policy?
- ▼ According to the policy you should not work on a machine without being trained. Were you trained and do you feel that it was adequate?
- ▼ Do you know who your supervisor is?
- ▼ Do you know who the injured person's supervisor is?
- ▼ Do you know who that supervisor's supervisor is?
- ▼ Do you know who is responsible for training?

▼ Do you know what that person's title is?

▼ Have you ever received any training from that person before?

▼ Have you ever asked for training before? If so, what were the results?

▼ Are you on the safety committee?

▼ If not, do you know who is on the safety committee?

▼ Do you know who the chairperson of the committee is?

▼ Do you ever see any minutes posted from the safety committee?

▼ Did you know that the safety committee met?

▼ How often do you think that the safety committee meets?

▼ What was the injured person's job?

▼ What other jobs do you know that injured person did within the company?

▼ What other job did you think he did in his work life?

▼ How much training do you think the person had at this company?

▼ Who do you think trained the person?

▼ Who supervised the person?

▼ Did the supervisor know the machine?

▼ Who do you think trained the supervisor?

▼ How long had the person operated the machine?

▼ Who ran the machine when the person was sick?

▼ How much training do you think this person got?

▼ Was the person a fast worker, or was this a low-key job for him to pass the time?

E. Sample Written Safety Program

Safety Policy

Safety Policy Statement: It is the policy of our company to protect the safety and health of our employees. Employees are our most valuable asset. It is our goal to eliminate injuries and property loss.

Management: It is the responsibility of our management to prevent accidents and injuries, to provide direction and support relative to safety procedures and job training, and to minimize—if not eliminate—job hazards. We must keep fully informed on health and safety in order to maintain an effective program. Workers are strongly encouraged to help managers in these endeavors.

Supervision: Supervisors are directly responsible for the safe work habits and job training of our workers. Supervisors must enforce company rules and take immediate corrective action to eliminate hazardous conditions. They shall not permit safety to be sacrificed for any reason.

Safety Committee: The safety committee consists of managers and employees strongly interested in the safety and health of all employees. The committee is responsible for recommendations on improving the safety of the workplace. It has been charged with the responsibility of identifying hazards, suggesting corrective actions, and developing accident investigation procedures.

Employees: Each employee, *regardless of position* within the company, is expected to cooperate in all aspects of the company's safety and health program. Our company safety program requires the following:

1. Immediately report all accidents to your supervisor. Note: The size of the accident is immaterial. We can always learn from them.
2. Immediately report all hazardous conditions or other safety concerns to your supervisor.
3. Wear the appropriate and/or required personal protective equipment.
4. Lock out or tag out any questionable equipment (equipment with inadequate or broken guards, frayed cords, overly worn components, etc.)

Each employee has a personal responsibility for his own safety as well as the safety of coworkers. If everyone is doing what is necessary to ensure workplace safety, we will all benefit. Speed is no substitute for safety.

General Safety Rules

1. Employees will report all injuries immediately to the person in charge. No employee shall go to a physician for treatment of any on-the-job injury without authorization from the office or supervisor except under emergency conditions. Injuries not reported before leaving the shift will result in any subsequent claim being questioned, thus jeopardizing rights to compensation. All employees are required to cooperate fully in the event of an accident investigation. An employee working in an unsafe manner, violating safety policies, or posing a threat to himself or others will be warned of the danger. His supervisor will indicate what corrective measures he is required to take. He will sign a Consent to Corrective Measures. A written notice of policy violation will be placed in his personnel file. Subsequent warnings will result in suspension or termination. All employees are re-

quired to attend safety meetings as called by their supervisors. Safety recommendations from employees are encouraged.

2. The use of intoxicating liquor or drugs on the job, or reporting to work under the influence of intoxicants, is strictly prohibited.

3. Protective equipment must be worn when required on specific jobs. Any deficiency in the required protective equipment must be reported to the supervisor immediately. Examples: Eye protection will be worn by workers exposed to flying objects. Steel-toe safety boots will be worn at all times unless authorized. Hearing protection will be worn during the use of any power equipment.

4. Only authorized persons shall operate machinery or equipment. A worker shall not operate a machine unless all guards are in good working order. Questionable equipment should immediately be brought to the supervisor's attention.

5. Supervisors must lock out or tag out dangerous equipment so that it will not operate. No worker shall ignore, remove, deface, or destroy any warning signs or interfere with any form of accident prevention device.

All employees shall promptly correct any unsafe condition, practice, or equipment. No employee shall work alone in a situation where the work might be dangerous. If you are in doubt, consult your supervisor.

F. Sample Hazardous Communications Program

The following is a sample program for you to use as a guideline in developing a Hazardous Communications Program for your company.

General Information

The management of "Company X" is committed to the prevention of incidents or happenings which result in injury and/or illness and to compliance with all applicable federal and state health and safety rules. Therefore, we require that management spare no effort in providing a safe and healthful work environment for all employees. All levels of supervision are accountable for the health and safety of those employees under their direction, and through this written hazard communication program, share assigned responsibility to ensure performance under that responsibility.

In order to comply with Occupational Health and Safety Code Hazardous Communication, the following Hazardous Communication Program has been established for "Company

X." All company divisions and sections are included in this program. The written program will be available from the personnel department for any interested employees. We, the management of "Company X," will meet the requirements of this rule as follows:

Container Labeling

The managers of "Company X" will verify all containers received for use. It is the policy of this company that no container will be released for use until the following are performed:

- ▼ The container is labeled as to the contents.
- ▼ The appropriate hazardous warning is noted.
- ▼ The manufacturer's name and address are recorded.

The supervisor in each section will ensure that all secondary containers are labeled with either an extra copy of the original manufacturer's label or with the "central stores" generic labels, which have identification and hazardous warning blocks. For help with labeling, see our safety and health officer.

Material Safety Data Sheets (MSDSs)

Copies of MSDSs for all hazardous materials to which employees of this Company may be exposed will be kept in the personnel and the safety offices. MSDSs will be available to all employees in their work and for review during each work shift. If MSDSs are not available or new hazardous materials in use do not have an MSDS, immediately contact the safety officer.

Employee Information and Training

Prior to starting work, each new employee of "Company X" will attend a health and safety orientation and will receive information and training on the following:

- ▼ An overview of the OSHA Act requirements for hazardous communication rules.

- Chemicals, gases, and other hazardous materials present in their workplace operations.
- Location and availability of our written hazardous substances program.
- Physical and health effects of the hazardous chemicals.
- Methods and techniques to determine the presence or release of hazardous chemicals.
- How to prevent exposure to hazardous substances through work practices.
- How to reduce exposure through use of personal protective equipment.
- Steps the company has taken to reduce or prevent exposure to these hazardous substances.
- Safety emergency procedures to follow if the employee is exposed to these chemicals.
- How to read labels and review MSDSs to obtain appropriate hazardous information.

After attending the training class, each employee will sign a form to verify they attended the training, received our written materials, and understood this Company's policies on hazardous communication.

Prior to a new hazardous material's being introduced into any section of this Company, each employee of that section will be given information as outlined above. The safety officer is responsible for ensuring that MSDSs on any new hazardous substance are available.

Hazardous Chemicals/Substance List

The following is a list of all known hazardous substances used by our employees. More information on each chemical noted is available by reviewing MSDSs located in the personnel and safety departments.

- Hazardous chemical
- Where it is used
- Where it is stored
- How and when it is used (e.g., in what processes)

Hazardous Nonroutine Tasks

Periodically, employees must perform hazardous nonroutine tasks. Before starting work on such projects, each affected employee will be given information by the section supervisor about the hazardous chemicals to which they may be exposed during such activity. This information will include:

- ▾ Specific chemical or gas hazards
- ▾ Protective and safety measures employees can take
- ▾ Measures the company has taken to reduce the hazards

Examples of nonroutine tasks performed by employees of this company are: [a list follows identifying the task, the hazardous chemical involved, and chemicals and gases in pipes].

Work activities are often performed by employees in areas where chemicals or gases are transferred through pipes. Prior to starting work in these areas, employees will contact the safety officer for information regarding:

- ▾ The chemical or gas in the pipes
- ▾ The insulation materials on the pipe
- ▾ Potential hazards
- ▾ Safety precautions to be taken

Outside Contractors

It is the responsibility of the safety officer to provide contractors with the following information:

- ▾ Hazardous chemicals to which they may be exposed while on the job site
- ▾ Procedures for obtaining MSDS information
- ▾ Precautions employees may take to lessen the possibility of exposure by using appropriate protective measures and an explanation of the labeling system used

In addition, it is the responsibility of the safety officer to identify and obtain MSDSs for the chemicals the contractor is bringing into the workplace.

G. Sample Job Hazard Analysis

Job Title: Waxing floor
Job Location: Main office area

Step 1: Select work area.
Hazard: Inadequate ventilation could create toxic fume problem.
Procedure: All areas must be checked for proper ventilation by supervisor before work begins. Use and sign floor conditioning check sheet to ensure proper materials.

Step 2: Transport equipment and supplies to work area.
Hazard: Improper tools and materials could cause delay. Some waxes present fire hazards. Certain surfaces are damaged by specific conditioning materials.
Procedure: Refer to floor conditioning check sheet for directions. Follow fire safety practices on check sheet with waxes indicated.

Step 3: Clear work area.
Hazard: Mixing furniture could disrupt office practices. Furniture handling presents foot and back injury exposure.

The information in this section of Resources and Checklists comes from the Cascade Employers Association and is used with permission.

Procedure: Use color coding system on all furniture. Use special lifting dollies on all furniture except chairs. Approved foot protection must be worn.

Step 4: Prepare work surface.
Hazard: Initial scrubbing could present slipping hazards.
Procedure: Rope off area being scrubbed. Place caution signs. Wear nonslip shoe covers.

Step 5: Remove old wax.
Hazard: Wax remover can cause slipping hazards. Remover may be toxic to breathe or touch.
Procedure: Rope off area being worked. Set up caution signs. Properly ventilate as directed. Wear protective equipment as indicated on checklist.

Step 6: Apply wax.
Hazard: Wax could present a fire hazard. Wax may be toxic to skin. Improper wax on surface could present slippery condition. Wax may be toxic to breathe. Wet wax can be slippery.
Procedure: Follow fire precautions and PPE listed on checklist. Ventilate as directed. Rope off area being waxed. Set up caution signs. Use wax indicated on checklist.

Step 7: Buff wax.
Hazard: Buffing machinery could cause foot injury.
Procedure: Follow job instruction for use on checklist. Wear foot protection.

Step 8: Realign work area.
Hazard: Moving furniture could disrupt offices and present foot and back injury exposure.
Procedure: Follow color code pattern to realign pieces. Use dollies on all heavy furniture.

Step 9: Return equipment and supplies.
Hazard: Equipment improperly returned can cause disruption in work. Empty cans can create housekeeping and fire problems.
Procedure: return everything to its proper place. Discard containers in outside dumpster.

H. Sample Equipment-Specific Guidelines

A safety program, to be complete, would require dozens of definitions and guidelines similar to what follows.

Explosive actuated fastening tools Class 1. These are explosive-actuated fastening tools that are actuated by explosives or any similar means and propel a stud, pin, fastener, or other object for the purpose of affixing it by penetration to any other object. They are used in our facility to attach widgets to thingamajigs.

Note: For definition purposes, these are not the explosive-actuated fastening tools that are used for attaching objects to soft construction materials, such as wood, plaster, tar, dry wallboard, and the like, or to stud welding equipment. Those tools are defined under Class 2.

Operating guidelines for explosive-actuated fastening tools Class 1 are as follows:

▼ Before using this tool, the operator shall inspect it to determine to his satisfaction that it is clean, that all moving parts operate freely, and that the barrel is free from obstructions.

▼ When a tool develops a defect during use, the operator shall immediately cease to use it until it is properly repaired.

▼ Tools shall not be loaded until just prior to the intended firing time. Neither loaded nor empty tools are to be pointed at any workers.

▼ No tools shall be loaded unless being prepared for immediate use, nor shall an unattended tool be left loaded.

▼ In case of a misfire, the operator shall hold the tool in the operating position for at least 30 seconds. The operator shall then try to operate the tool a second time. He then shall wait another 30 seconds, holding the tool in the operating position; then he shall proceed to remove the explosive load in strict accordance with the manufacturer's instructions.

▼ A tool shall never be left unattended in a place where it would be available to unauthorized persons.

▼ Fasteners shall not be driven into very hard or brittle materials including, but not limited to, cast iron, glazed tile, surface-hardened steel, glass block, live rock, brick, or hollow tile.

▼ Driving into materials easily penetrated shall be avoided unless such materials are backed by a substance that will prevent the pin or fastener from passing completely through and creating a flying-missile hazard on the other side.

▼ Fasteners shall not be driven directly into materials such as brick or concrete closer than 3 inches from the unsupported edge or corner, or into steel surfaces closer than $1/2$ inch from the unsupported edge or corner, unless a special guard, fixture, or jig is used (*exception:* low-velocity tools may drive no closer than 2 inches from an edge in concrete or $1/4$ inch in steel). When fastening others materials, such as a 2- by 4-inch wood section to a concrete surface, it is permissible to drive a fastener of no greater than $7/32$-inch shank diameter not closer than 2 inches from the unsupported edge or corner of the work surface.

▼ Fasteners shall not be driven through existing holes unless a positioning guide is used to secure accurate alignment.

▼ No fastener shall be driven into a spalled area caused by an unsatisfactory fastening.

▼ Tools shall not be used in an explosive or flammable atmosphere.

▼ All tools shall be used with the correct shield, guard, or attachment recommended by the manufacturer.

▼ Any tool found not in proper working order shall be immediately removed from service. The tool shall be inspected at regular intervals and shall be repaired in accordance with the manufacturer's specifications.

I. Direct and Indirect Causes of Accidents

The direct cause is whatever unsafe act (doing something or failing to do something) brought about the accident.

The following are examples of direct causes:

- Struck against
- Struck by
- Fall from
- Fall on
- Caught in
- Caught on
- Caught between or under
- Rubbed or abraded
- Overexertion or overstress
- Bodily reaction or movement
- Contact with temperature extremes
- Contact with toxic, caustic, or noxious substances
- Contact with radiation
- Contact with electric current
- Contact with sound

The material in this section of Resources and Checklists comes from the Cascade Employees Association and is used with permission.

▾ Motor vehicle, ship, and aircraft impacts

Indirect causes are unsafe acts or unsafe conditions that relate to the direct cause of the accident.

Examples of unsafe acts are:

▾ Servicing equipment in motion
▾ Failure to warn or secure
▾ Making safety devices inoperative
▾ Operating or working at unsafe speed
▾ Taking unsafe position or posture
▾ Unsafe placing, mixing, or combining
▾ Improper use of equipment
▾ Improper use of hands or body parts
▾ Substandard practices such as horseplay or failure to wear proper attire

Examples of unsafe conditions include:

▾ Hazardous methods or procedures
▾ Placement hazards
▾ Inadequate guarding
▾ Hazardous outside work environments
▾ Dress or apparel condition hazards
▾ Defects

Some examples of basic causes include:

▾ Inadequate codes and standards
▾ Lack of policy
▾ Failure of supervisors to perform their duties
▾ Lack of enforcement
▾ Faulty design
▾ Inadequate maintenance
▾ Inadequate training
▾ Lack of safety training

J. Job Redesign

Sometimes even simple changes in a task or its components can make a job safer or appropriate for a wider range of workers. According to Linda Atwill (*Business Insurance News,* Fall 1995), the following recommendations can be used for guidance when designing manual material handling tasks.

Minimizing Significant Body Motions

▼ Eliminate the need to bend by:
  —Using lift tables, work dispensers, and similar aids.
  —Raising the work level to an appropriate height.
  —Lowering the worker.
  —Providing all material at work level.
  —Keeping materials at work level.
▼ Eliminate the need to twist by:
  —Providing all materials and tools in front of the worker.
  —Using conveyors, chutes . . . or turntables to change direction of material flow.
  —Providing adjustable swivel chairs for seated workers.
  —Providing sufficient work space for the whole body to turn.
  —Improving the layout of the work area.
▼ Eliminate the need to reach by:
  —Providing the tools and machine controls close to the worker.

—Placing the workplace materials as near the worker as possible.
—Reducing the size of cartons or pallets being loaded.
—Allowing the worker to walk around the pallets or rotate them.
—Reducing the size of objects being handled.
—Allowing the object to be kept close to the body.

Reduce Lifting and Lowering Forces

▼ Eliminate the need to lift or lower manually by:
—Using lift tables, lift trucks, barrel dumpers, and other mechanical aids.
—Raising the work level.
—Lowering the operator.
—Using gravity dumps and chutes.
▼ Reduce the weight of the object by:
—Reducing the size of the object.
—Reducing the capacity of containers.
—Reducing the weight of the container.
—Reducing the load in the container.
—Reducing the number of objects lifted or lowered at one time.
▼ Increase the weight of the object so that it must be handled mechanically by:
—Using the unit load concept (such as bins rather than smaller totes).
—Using palletized loads.
▼ Reduce the hand distance by:
—Changing the shape of the object.
—Providing grips or handles.
—Providing better access to the object.
—Improving the layout of the work area.

Provide Pushing and Pulling Forces

▼ Eliminate the need to push or pull by:
—Using powered conveyors.
—Using powered trucks.

—Using slides and chutes.
- ▼ Reduce the required force by:
  —Reducing the weight of the load.
  —Using nonpowered conveyors, air bearings, ball caster tables, monorails.
  —Using the four-wheel hand trucks and dollies with large diameter casters.
  —Providing good maintenance of floor surfaces, hand trucks, etc.
  —Training surfaces to reduce friction.
  —Using air cylinder pushers or pullers.
- ▼ Reduce the distance of push or pull by:
  —Improving the layout of the work area.
  —Relocating the production or storage area.

Reduce Carrying Forces

- ▼ Eliminate the need to carry by converting to pushing or pulling by:
  —Using conveyors, air bearings, ball caster tables, monorails, slides, chutes.
  —Using lift trucks, two-wheel hand trucks, four-wheel hand trucks, dollies.
- ▼ Reduce the weight of the object by:
  —Reducing the size of the object.
  —Reducing the capacity of containers.
  —Reducing the weight of the container.
  —Reducing the load in the container.
  —Reducing the number of objects lifted or lowered at one time.
- ▼ Reduce the distance by:
  —Improving the layout of the work area.
  —Relocating production or storage areas.

K. Sample Sign-Off Form: Training Record for Hazardous Communications

This is to certify that I have been trained and informed on the hazards and precautions associated with the use of hazardous chemicals in my work as required in the company's written hazardous communication program.

To confirm my understanding of such training and instructions, [name] reviewed them with me and he/she indicated his/her satisfaction by checking the box before each of the topics listed below:

☐ Overview of the requirements contained in the hazardous communication rules.

☐ Chemicals present in my workplace operations.

☐ Locations and availability of our written hazard communication program and the Material Safety Data Sheets for the hazardous chemicals.

☐ Physical and health effects of these hazardous chemicals.

☐ Methods and observation techniques used to determine the presence or release of hazardous chemicals in my work area.

☐ How to lessen or prevent exposure to these hazardous chemicals through usage of control/work practices and personal protective equipment.

☐ Steps the company has taken to lessen or prevent exposure to these chemicals.

☐ Safety emergency procedures to follow in the event of exposure to these chemicals.

☐ How to read container labels, review and interpret Material Safety Data Sheets to obtain appropriate hazard information.

_____

Employee's Name

_____

Date

Attested:

_____

Trainer

_____

Date

Note to employee: This form will be made part of your personnel file. It should be considered a legal document. Please read and understand its contents before signing.

L. Sample Drug and Alcohol Policy

Our company is committed to performing work of the highest possible quality, providing excellent services to our customers, and providing a safe and productive work environment for our employees.

We expect and require the support of all of our employees in meeting these commitments. We recognize that employees who are unable to do their best work in a safe manner due to the effects of drugs or alcohol interfere with these commitments.

Each employee is expected and required to report for work on time and in appropriate mental and physical condition to work safely and effectively. Working, reporting for work, or engaging in any activity on the company's behalf with alcohol or a controlled substance in your system is prohibited.

The use, sale, transfer, or possession of any controlled substance or alcoholic beverage on company premises, in company vehicles, or while conducting any business on the company's behalf is prohibited.

Each employee must report to his or her immediate supervisor the use of any prescription or over-the-counter medication that may affect the employee's ability to perform job duties safely and effectively. It is the employee's responsibility to determine whether any prescribed drug or other medication may impair job performance. Employees are also required to provide medical authorization to work upon request.

Each employee is required to submit to drug and/or alcohol testing when required, to complete related paperwork, and to participate and cooperate fully in specimen collection procedures. Violation of the drug and alcohol policy will subject an employee to disciplinary action up to and including discharge.

Drug testing will be required in the following situations:

1. When an employee has been determined by the company to have caused or contributed to an accident resulting in injury or property damage.
2. When there is reasonable suspicion, as determined by the company, that an employee may be in violation of the drug and alcohol policy.
3. Preemployment, following a conditional offer of employment; this is mandatory.

If you think you have a problem with drugs or alcohol, we encourage you to share your concerns with the owner, who will assist you in the process of obtaining an evaluation. No employee coming forward voluntarily for such help will be subject to disciplinary action solely as a result of seeking assistance. If you are referred for treatment requiring time away from work, you may be asked to sign and follow a Return-to-Work Agreement.

After any disciplinary action imposed following a positive test that determined a violation of this policy, an employee may remain eligible for continuing employment. If eligible, an employee will be required to sign and follow, as a condition of continuing employment, a "Last-Chance" Agreement. Please ask for assistance if in need of further explanation.

M. Self-Inspection Checklists

These checklists can help you conduct an effective self-inspection. Certain checklists can also help you prepare for an OSHA and/or routine internal inspection.

Employer Posting

☐ Are any OSHA-required materials posted in a prominent location where employees will see them?

☐ Are emergency telephone numbers posted where they can be readily used in case of emergency?

☐ Where employees may be exposed to any toxic substances or harmful physical agents, has appropriate information concerning employee access to medical and exposure records and Material Safety Data Sheets been posted or otherwise made readily available to affected employees?

☐ Are signs regarding exits from buildings, room capacity, floor loading, exposure to X-ray, microwave, or other harmful radiation or substances posted where required?

Record Keeping

☐ Are all occupational injuries and illnesses, except minor injuries requiring only first aid, being recorded and reported as required?

☐ Are copies of all records preserved and maintained for the mandated length of time (in some cases, up to forty years)?

☐ Are employee medical records and records of employee exposures to hazardous substances or harmful physical agents current?

☐ Are operating permits and records current for such items as elevators, pressure vessels, and liquefied petroleum gas tanks?

☐ Are employee safety and health training records maintained?

☐ Is documentation of safety inspections and corrections maintained?

Injury- and Illness-Prevention Plan

☐ Do you have top management commitment?

☐ Have you established labor and management accountability?

☐ Do you have a system in place for hazard identification and control?

☐ Do you investigate all incidents and accidents?

☐ Do you encourage employee involvement in health and safety matters?

☐ Do you provide occupational safety and health training for your workers and supervisors?

☐ Do you perform periodic evaluations of the plan?

Medical Services and First Aid

☐ Has an emergency medical plan been developed?

☐ Are emergency telephone numbers posted?

☐ Are first aid kits easily accessible to each work area, with necessary supplies available, and periodically inspected and replenished as needed?

☐ Are means provided for quick drenching or flushing of the eyes and body in areas where caustic or corrosive liquids or materials are handled?

Safety Committees

☐ Do you have an active safety committee with equal numbers of management and employees?

☐ Are records kept documenting safety and health training for each employee by name or other identifier, training dates, type(s) of training, and training provider?

☐ Does the committee meet at least monthly (quarterly for office-type environments)?

☐ Is a written record of safety committee meetings distributed to affected employees and maintained for division review?

☐ Does the safety committee conduct quarterly hazard identification surveys?

☐ Does the committee review results of periodic, scheduled work site inspections?

☐ Does the committee review accident and near-miss investigations and, where necessary, submit recommendations for prevention of future incidents?

☐ Does the committee involve all workers in the safety and health program?

☐ Are safety committee minutes kept for three years, and are each month's minutes posted?

☐ Has your safety committee developed an accident investigation procedure?

☐ Has the committee reviewed your safety and health program and made recommendations for possible improvements?

☐ Have committee members been trained and instructed in safety committee purpose and operation, methods of conducting meetings, OSHA rules that apply to the workplace, hazard identification, and accident investigation principles?

Fire Protection

☐ Do you have a written fire prevention plan?

☐ Does your plan describe the type of fire protection equipment and/or systems?

☐ Have you established practices and procedures to control potential fire hazards and ignition sources?

☐ Are employees aware of the fire hazards of the materials and processes to which they are exposed?

- [ ] If you have a fire alarm system, is it tested at least annually?
- [ ] Are sprinkler heads protected by metal guards when exposed to physical damage?
- [ ] Is proper clearance maintained below sprinkler heads?
- [ ] Are portable fire extinguishers provided in adequate numbers and types?
- [ ] Are fire extinguishers mounted in readily accessible locations?
- [ ] Are fire extinguishers recharged regularly and then noted on the inspection tag?
- [ ] Are employees trained in the use of extinguishers and fire protection systems?

Personal Protective Equipment and Clothing

- [ ] Has there been an assessment of the hazards that might require PPE, including a review of injuries?
- [ ] Has the assessment been verified through written certification?
- [ ] Does it identify the workplace evaluated?
- [ ] Has trained been provided to each employee required to wear PPE?
- [ ] Has the training been verified through written certification?
- [ ] Are protective goggles or face shields provided and worn when there is any danger of flying material or caustic or corrosive materials?
- [ ] Are approved safety glasses required to be worn at all times in areas where there is risk of eye injury?
- [ ] Are protective gloves, aprons, shields, or other protection provided against cuts, corrosive liquids, and chemicals?
- [ ] Are hard hats provided and worn where danger of falling objects exists?
- [ ] Are hard hats inspected periodically for damage to the shell and suspension system?
- [ ] Are approved respirators provided for regular or emergency use where needed?
- [ ] Is there a written respirator program?

☐ Are the respirators inspected before and after each use?

☐ Is a written record kept of all inspection dates and findings?

☐ Have all employees been trained in adequate work procedures, use and maintenance of protective clothing, and proper use of equipment when cleaning up spilled toxic or other hazardous materials or liquids?

☐ Is a spill kit available to clean up spilled toxic or hazardous materials?

☐ Where employees are exposed to conditions that could cause foot injury, are safety shoes required to be worn?

☐ Is all protective equipment maintained in a sanitary condition and ready to use?

☐ Do you have eyewash facilities and a quick-drench shower within a work area where employees are exposed to caustic or corrosive materials?

☐ When lunches are eaten on the premises, are they eaten in areas where there is no exposure to toxic materials or other health hazards?

☐ Is protection against the effects of occupational noise exposure provided when sound levels exceed those of the OSHA noise and hearing conservation standard?

General Work Environment

☐ Are all work sites clean and orderly?

☐ Are work surfaces kept dry, or are appropriate means taken to ensure the surfaces are slip resistant?

☐ Are all spilled materials or liquids cleaned up immediately?

☐ Is combustible scrap, debris, and waste stored safely and removed from the work site promptly?

☐ Are covered metal waste cans used for oily and paint-soaked waste?

☐ Are the minimum required number of toilets and washing facilities provided?

☐ Are all toilets and washing facilities clean and sanitary?

☐ Are all work areas adequately lighted?

Walkways

- [ ] Are aisles and passageways kept clear, and are they at least 22 inches wide?
- [ ] Are aisles and walkways appropriately marked?
- [ ] Are wet surfaces covered with nonslip materials?
- [ ] Are openings or holes in the floors or other treading surfaces repaired or otherwise made safe?
- [ ] Is there safe clearance for walking in aisles where vehicles are operating?
- [ ] Are materials or equipment stored so sharp objects cannot obstruct the walkway?
- [ ] Are changes of direction or elevations readily identifiable?
- [ ] Are aisles or walkways that pass near moving or operating machinery, welding operations, or similar operations arranged so employees will not be subjected to potential hazards?
- [ ] Is adequate headroom (or at least 6.5 feet) provided for the entire length of any walkway?
- [ ] Are standard guardrails provided wherever aisle or walkway surfaces are elevated more than 4 feet above any adjacent floor or the ground?
- [ ] Are bridges provided over conveyors and similar hazards?

Floor and Wall Openings

- [ ] Are floor holes or openings guarded by a cover, guardrail, or equivalent on all sides (except at entrance to stairways or ladders)?
- [ ] Are toe boards installed around the edges of a permanent floor opening (where persons may pass below the opening)?
- [ ] Are skylight screens of such construction and mounting that they will withstand a load of at least 200 pounds?
- [ ] Is the glass in windows, doors, and glass walls (which may be subject to human impact) of sufficient thickness and type for all conditions or use?
- [ ] Are grates or similar covers over floor openings, such as floor drains, of such design that foot traffic or rolling equipment will not be caught by the grate spacing?
- [ ] Are unused portions of service pits and pits not actually in

use either covered or protected by guardrails or equivalent?

Stairs and Stairways

☐ Are standard stair rails and handrails present on all stairways having four or more risers?
☐ Are all stairways at least 22 inches wide?
☐ Do stairs have at least a 6.5-foot overhead clearance?
☐ Do stairs angle no more than 50 degrees and no less than 30 degrees?
☐ Are step risers on stairs uniform from top to bottom, with no riser spacing greater than 7.5 inches?
☐ Are steps on stairs and stairways designed or provided with a surface that renders them slip resistant?
☐ Are stairway handrails located between 30 and 34 inches above the leading edge of stair treads?
☐ Do stairway handrails have at least 3 inches of clearance between handrails and the wall or surface they are mounted on?
☐ Are stairway handrails capable of withstanding a load of 200 pounds applied in any direction?
☐ Where stairs or stairways exit directly into any area where vehicles may be operated, are adequate barriers and warnings provided to prevent employees from stepping into the path of traffic?

Elevated Surfaces

☐ Are signs posted, when appropriate, showing elevated floor load capacity?
☐ Are elevated surfaces (more than 4 feet above the floor or ground) provided with standard guardrails?
☐ Are all elevated surfaces (beneath which people or machinery could be exposed to falling objects) provided with standard toe boards?
☐ Is a permanent means of access/egress provided to elevated work areas?
☐ Is material on elevated surfaces piled, stacked, or racked

in a manner to prevent it from tipping, falling, collapsing, rolling, or spreading?

☐ Are dock boards or bridge plates used when transferring materials between docks and trucks or railcars?

☐ When in use, are dock boards or bridge plates secured in place?

Exits

☐ Are all exits marked with an exit sign and illuminated by a reliable light source?

☐ Are the directions to exits, if not immediately apparent, marked with visible signs?

☐ Are doors, passageways, or stairways that are neither exits nor access to exits and which could be mistaken for exits appropriately marked "not an exit," or "to basement," "storeroom," and the like?

☐ Are exit signs provided with the word *exit* in lettering at least 6 inches high with the stroke of the lettering at least ¾ inch wide?

☐ Are exit doors side hinged?

☐ Are all exits kept free of obstructions and unlocked?

☐ Are at least two means of egress provided from elevated platforms, pits, or rooms where the absence of a second exit would increase the risk of injury from hot, poisonous, corrosive, suffocating, flammable, or explosive substances?

☐ Are there sufficient exits to permit prompt escape in case of emergency?

☐ Are the number of exits from each floor of a building and the number of exits from the building itself appropriate for the building occupancy load?

☐ When workers must exit through glass doors, storm doors, and such, are the doors fully tempered and do they meet safety requirements for human impact?

Exit Doors

☐ Are doors that are required to serve as exits designed and constructed so that the way of exit travel is obvious and direct?

☐ Are windows (which could be mistaken for exit doors) made inaccessible by barriers or railing?

☐ Are exit doors able to open from the direction of exit travel without the use of a key or any special knowledge or effort?

☐ Is a revolving, sliding, or overhead door prohibited from serving as a required exit door?

☐ When panic hardware is installed on a required exit door, will it allow the door to open by applying a force of 15 pounds or less in the direction of the exit traffic?

☐ Are doors on cold-storage rooms provided with an inside release mechanism that will release the latch and open the door even if it is padlocked or otherwise locked on the outside?

☐ Where exit doors open directly onto any street, alley, or other area where vehicles may be operated, are adequate barriers and warnings provided to prevent employees from stepping directly into the path of traffic?

☐ Are doors that swing in both directions and are located between rooms where there is frequent traffic provided with viewing panels in each door?

Portable Ladders

☐ Are all ladders maintained in good condition, joints between steps and side rails tight, all hardware and fittings securely attached, and movable parts operating freely without binding or undue play?

☐ Are nonslip safety feet provided on each ladder, including metal or rung ladders?

☐ Are ladder rungs and steps free of grease and oil?

☐ Is it prohibited to place a ladder in front of doors opening toward the ladder except when the door is blocked open, locked, or guarded?

☐ Is it prohibited to place ladders on boxes, barrels, or other unstable bases to obtain additional height?

☐ Are employees instructed to face the ladder when ascending/descending?

☐ Are employees prohibited from using ladders that are broken, missing steps, rungs or cleats, broken side rails, or other faulty equipment?

☐ Are employees instructed not to use the top step of ordinary stepladders as a step?

☐ When portable rung ladders are used to gain access to elevated platforms, roofs, and the like, does the ladder always extend at least 3 feet above the elevated surface?

☐ Is it required that when portable rung or cleat-type ladders are used, the base is so placed that slipping will not occur, or it is lashed or otherwise held in place?

☐ Are portable and metal ladders legibly marked with signs reading CAUTION: DO NOT USE AROUND ELECTRICAL EQUIPMENT or equivalent wording?

☐ Are the rungs of ladders uniformly spaced at 12 inches, center to center?

Hand Tools and Equipment

☐ Are all tools and equipment (both company and employee owned) in good working condition?

☐ Are hand tools such as chisels or punches (which develop mushroomed heads during use) reconditioned or replaced as necessary?

☐ Are broken or fractured handles on hammers, axes, or similar equipment replaced promptly?

☐ Are appropriate handles used on files and similar tools?

☐ Are appropriate safety glasses, face shields, and similar equipment used while using hand tools or equipment that might produce flying materials or be subject to breakage?

☐ Are jacks checked periodically to ensure that they are in good operating condition?

☐ Are tool handles wedged tightly in the head of all tools?

☐ Are tool cutting edges kept sharp so the tool will move smoothly without binding or skipping?

☐ Is eye and face protection used when driving hardened or tempered tools, bits, or nails?

Portable (Power-Operated) Tools and Equipment

☐ Are grinders, saws, and similar equipment provided with appropriate safety guards?

☐ Are power tools used with the shield or guard recommended by the manufacturer?

☐ Are portable circular saws equipped with guards above and below the base shoe?

☐ Are circular saw guards checked to ensure guarding of the lower blade portion?

☐ Are rotating or moving parts of equipment guarded to prevent physical contact?

☐ Are all cord-connected, electrically operated tools and equipment effectively grounded or of the approved double-insulated type?

☐ Are effective guards in place over belts, pulleys, chains, and sprockets on equipment such as concrete mixers, air compressors, and the like?

☐ Are portable fans provided with full guards having openings of ½ inch or less?

☐ Is hoisting equipment available and used for lifting heavy objects, and are hoist ratings and characteristics appropriate for the task?

☐ Are ground-fault circuit interrupters (provided on all temporary electrical 15 and 20 ampere circuits) used during periods of construction?

☐ Are pneumatic and hydraulic hoses on power-operated tools checked regularly for deterioration or damage?

Abrasive Wheel Equipment Grinders

☐ Is the work rest used and kept adjusted to within ⅛ inch of the wheel?

☐ Is the adjustable tongue on the top side of the grinder used and kept adjusted to within ¼ inch of the wheel?

☐ Do side guards cover the spindle, nut, flange, and 75 percent of the wheel diameter?

☐ Are bench and pedestal grinders permanently mounted?

☐ Are goggles or face shields always worn when grinding?

☐ Is the maximum rotations per minute (rpm) rating of each abrasive wheel compatible with the rpm rating of the grinder motor?

☐ Are fixed or permanently mounted grinders connected to

their electrical supply system with metallic conduit or by
another permanent wiring method?

☐ Does each grinder have an individual on/off switch?

☐ Is each electrically operated grinder effectively grounded?

☐ Before mounting new abrasive wheels, are they visually
inspected and ring tested?

☐ Are dust collectors and powered exhausts provided on
grinders used in operations that produce large amounts of
dust?

☐ To prevent coolant from splashing workers, are splash
guards mounted on grinders that use coolant?

☐ Is cleanliness maintained around grinders?

Machine Guarding

☐ Is there an employee training program for safe methods of
machine operation?

☐ Is there adequate supervision to ensure that employees
are following safe machine operating procedures?

☐ Is there a regular program of safety inspection for machinery and equipment?

☐ Is all machinery and equipment clean and properly maintained?

☐ Is sufficient clearance provided around and between machines to allow for safe operations, set-up and servicing,
material handling, and waste removal?

☐ Is equipment and machinery securely placed and anchored
when necessary to prevent tipping or other movement that
could result in personal injury?

☐ Is there a power shut-off switch within reach of the operator's position at each machine?

☐ Are the noncurrent-carrying metal parts of electrically operated machines bonded and grounded?

☐ Are foot-operated switches guarded or arranged to prevent
accidental actuation by personnel or falling objects?

☐ Are manually operated valves and switches (controlling
the operation of equipment and machines) clearly identified and readily accessible?

☐ Are all emergency stop buttons colored red?

☐ Are all pulleys and belts that are located within 7 feet of the floor or working level properly guarded?

☐ Are all moving chains and gears properly guarded?

☐ Are methods provided to protect the operator and other employees in the machine area from hazards created at the point of operation, nip points, rotating parts, flying chips, and sparks?

☐ Are machinery guards secured and arranged so they do not offer a hazard in their use?

☐ If special hand tools are used for placing and removing material, do they protect the operator's hands?

☐ Are revolving drums, barrels, and containers (required to be guarded by an enclosure interlocked with the drive mechanism so that revolution cannot occur) guarded?

☐ Do arbors and mandrels have firm and secure bearings, and are they free from play?

☐ Are provisions made to prevent machines from automatically starting when power is restored (following a power failure or shutdown)?

☐ Are machines constructed so as to be free from excessive vibration (when the largest size tool is mounted and run at full speed)?

☐ If machinery is cleaned with compressed air, is air pressure controlled and personal protective equipment or other safeguards used to protect operators and other workers from eye and body injury?

☐ Are fan blades protected with a guard having openings no larger than ½ inch when operating within 7 feet of the floor?

☐ Are saws used for ripping equipped with anti-kickback devices and spreaders?

☐ Are radial arm saws guarded and so arranged that the cutting head will gently return to the back of the table when released?

Lockout/Tagout Procedures

☐ Is all machinery or equipment (capable of movement) required to be deenergized or disengaged and locked out during cleaning, servicing, adjusting, or setting up operations?

☐ Is it prohibited to lock out control circuits in lieu of locking out main power disconnects?

☐ Are all equipment control valves provided with a means of lockout?

☐ Does the lockout/tagout procedure require that stored energy (e.g., mechanical, hydraulic, air) be released or blocked before equipment is locked out for repairs?

☐ Are appropriate employees provided with individually keyed personal safety locks?

☐ Are employees required to keep personal control of their key(s) while they have safety locks in use?

☐ Is it required that employees check the safety of the lockout by attempting to start up after making sure no one is exposed?

☐ Where the power disconnecting means for equipment does not also disconnect the electrical control circuit, are the appropriate electrical closures identified?

☐ Are means provided to ensure the control circuit can also be disconnected and locked out?

Welding, Cutting, and Brazing

☐ Are only authorized and trained personnel permitted to use welding, cutting, or brazing equipment?

☐ Are compressed gas cylinders regularly examined for signs of defect, deep rusting, or leakage?

☐ Are cylinders kept away from sources of heat?

☐ Is it prohibited to use cylinders as rollers or supports?

☐ Are empty cylinders appropriately marked, their valves closed, and valve protection caps placed on them?

☐ Are signs reading DANGER—NO SMOKING, MATCHES OR OPEN LIGHTS, or the equivalent, posted?

☐ Are cylinders, cylinder valves, couplings, regulators, hoses, and apparatus kept free of oily or greasy substances?

☐ Unless secured on special trucks, are regulators removed and valve protection caps put in place before moving cylinders?

☐ Do cylinders without fixed hand wheels have keys, handles, or nonadjustable wrenches on stem valves when in service?

☐ Are liquefied gases stored and shipped with the valve end up and with valve covers in place?

☐ Before a regulator is removed, is the valve closed, and then gas released from the regulator?

☐ Is open circuit (no load) voltage of arc welding and cutting machines as low as possible, and not in excess of the recommended limit?

☐ Are electrodes removed from the holders when not in use?

☐ Is it required that electric power to the welder be shut off when no one is in attendance?

☐ Is suitable fire extinguishing equipment available for immediate use?

☐ Is the welder forbidden to coil or loop welding electric cable around his/her body?

☐ Are work and electrode lead cable frequently inspected for wear and damage, and replaced when needed?

☐ Do means for connecting cable lengths have adequate insulation?

☐ When the object to be welded cannot be moved and fire hazards cannot be removed, are shields used to confine heat, sparks, and slag?

☐ Are fire watchers assigned when welding or cutting is performed in locations where a serious fire might develop?

☐ When welding is done on all metal walls, are precautions taken to protect combustibles on the other side?

☐ Before hot work begins, are drums, barrels, tanks, and other containers so thoroughly cleaned and tested that no substances remain that could explode, ignite, or produce toxic vapors?

☐ Do eye protection helmets, hand shields, and goggles meet appropriate standards?

☐ Are employees exposed to the hazards created by welding, cutting, or brazing operations protected with personal protective equipment and clothing?

☐ Is a check made for adequate ventilation in and where welding or cutting is performed?

☐ When working in confined spaces, are environmental monitoring tests taken and means provided for quick removal of welders in case of an emergency?

Compressors and Compressed Air

☐ Are compressors equipped with pressure relief valves and pressure gauges?

☐ Are compressor air intakes installed and equipped to ensure that only clean, uncontaminated air enters the compressor?

☐ Are air filters installed on the compressor intake?

☐ Are compressors operated and lubricated in accordance with the manufacturer's recommendations?

☐ Are safety devices on compressed air systems checked frequently?

☐ Before any repair work is done on the pressure systems of the compressor, is the pressure bled off and the system locked out?

☐ Are signs posted to warn of the automatic starting feature of the compressors?

☐ Is the belt drive system totally enclosed to provide protection on the front, back, top, and sides?

☐ Is it strictly prohibited to direct compressed air toward a person?

☐ Are employees prohibited from using compressed air (at over 29 psi) for cleaning purposes?

☐ Are employees prohibited from cleaning off clothing with compressed air?

☐ When using compressed air for cleaning, do employees use personal protective equipment?

☐ Are safety chains or other suitable locking devices used at couplings of high-pressure hose lines where a connection failure would create a hazard?

☐ Before compressed air is used to empty containers of liquid, is the safe working pressure of the container checked?

☐ When compressed air is used with abrasive blast cleaning equipment, is the operating valve a type that must be held open manually?

☐ Is it prohibited to use compressed air to clean up or move combustible dust, if such action could cause the dust to be suspended in the air and cause a fire or explosion?

☐ If plastic piping is used, is the plastic approved for airline service? (Some ABS is okay; PVC is not.)

Compressed Gas and Cylinders

☐ Are cylinders with water weight capacity over 30 pounds equipped (with means for connecting a valve protector or device or with a collar or recess) to protect the valve?

☐ Are cylinders legibly marked to clearly identify the gas contained?

☐ Are compressed gas cylinders stored in areas that are protected from external heat sources (such as flames impingement, intense radiant heat, electric arcs, or high-temperature lines)?

☐ Are cylinders located or stored in areas where they will not be damaged by passing or falling objects or be subject to tampering by unauthorized persons?

☐ Are cylinders stored or transported in a manner to prevent them from creating a hazard by tipping, falling, or rolling?

☐ Are cylinders containing liquefied fuel gas stored or transported in a position so that the safety relief device is always in direct contact with the vapor space in the cylinder?

☐ Are valve protectors always placed on cylinders when the cylinders are not in use or connected for use?

☐ Are all valves closed off before a cylinder is moved, when the cylinder is empty, and at the completion of each job?

☐ Are low-pressure fuel gas cylinders checked periodically for corrosion, general distortion, cracks, or any other defect that might indicate a weakness or render them unfit for service?

☐ Does the periodic check of low-pressure fuel gas cylinders include a close inspection of the bottom of each cylinder?

Industrial Trucks and Forklifts

☐ Are only trained personnel allowed to operate industrial trucks?

☐ Is substantial overhead protective equipment provided on high-lift rider equipment?

☐ Are the required lift truck operating rules posted and enforced, and is the capacity rating posted in plain view of the operator?

☐ Is directional lighting provided on each industrial truck that operates in an area with less than 2 foot-candles per square foot of general lighting?

☐ Does each industrial truck have a warning horn, whistle, gong, or other device that can be clearly heard above the normal noise in the area where operated?

☐ Are the brakes on each industrial truck capable of bringing the vehicle to a complete and safe stop when fully loaded?

☐ Will the industrial truck's parking brake effectively prevent the vehicle from moving when unattended?

☐ Are industrial trucks operating in areas where flammable gases or vapors, combustible dust, or ignitable fibers may be present in the atmosphere approved for such locations?

☐ Are motorized hand and hand-rider trucks so designed that the brakes are applied and power to the drive motor shuts off when the operator releases his/her grip on the device that controls the travel?

☐ Are industrial trucks with internal combustion engines (and operated in buildings or enclosed areas) carefully checked to ensure such operations do not cause harmful concentration of dangerous gases or fumes?

Spray Finishing Operations

☐ Is adequate ventilation ensured before spray operations are started?

☐ Is mechanical ventilation provided when spraying is performed in enclosed areas?

☐ When mechanical ventilation is provided during spraying operations, is it arranged so that it will not circulate contaminated air?

☐ Is the spray area free of hot surfaces?

☐ Is the spray area at least 20 feet from flames, sparks, operating electrical motors, and other ignition sources?

☐ Are the portable lamps used to illuminate spray areas suitable for use in a hazardous location?

☐ Is approved respiratory equipment provided and used during spraying operations?

☐ Do solvents used for cleaning have a flash point of 100 degrees Fahrenheit or more?

☐ Are fire control sprinkler heads kept clean?

☐ Are NO SMOKING signs posted in the spray areas, paint rooms, paint booths, and paint storage areas?

☐ Is the spray area kept clean of combustible residue?

☐ Are spray booths constructed of metal, masonry, or other substantial noncombustible material?

☐ Are spray booth floors and baffles noncombustible and easily cleaned?

☐ Is infrared drying apparatus kept out of the spray area during spraying operations?

☐ Is the spray booth completely ventilated before the drying apparatus is used? Is the electric drying apparatus properly grounded? Do all drying spaces have adequate ventilation?

☐ Are lighting fixtures for spray booths located outside the booth, and the interior lighted through sealed clear panels?

☐ Are the electric motors for exhaust fans placed outside booths or ducts?

☐ Are belts and pulleys inside the booth fully enclosed?

☐ Do ducts have access doors to allow cleaning?

Confined Spaces

☐ Is there a written permit confined-space program?

☐ Is the program available for inspection?

☐ Are confined spaces thoroughly emptied of any corrosive or hazardous substances, such as acids or caustics, before entry?

☐ Before entry, are all pipelines to a confined space containing inert, toxic, flammable, or corrosive materials valved off and blanked or disconnected and separated?

☐ Are all impellers, agitators, or other moving equipment inside confined spaces locked out if they present a hazard?

☐ Is either natural or mechanical ventilation provided prior to confined-space entry?

☐ Before entry, are appropriate atmospheric tests performed to check for oxygen deficiency, toxic substances, and explosive concentrations in the confined space?

☐ Is adequate lighting provided for the work being performed in the confined space?

☐ Is the atmosphere inside the confined space frequently tested or continuously monitored during the work process?

☐ Is there an attendant standing by outside the confined space, whose sole responsibility is to watch the work in progress, sound an alarm if necessary, and help render assistance?

☐ Is the attendant or other employees prohibited from entering the confined space without lifelines and respiratory equipment if there is an emergency?

☐ In addition to the attendant, is there at least one other trained rescuer in the vicinity?

☐ Are all rescuers appropriately trained and using approved, recently inspected equipment?

☐ Does all rescue equipment allow for lifting of employees vertically through a top opening?

☐ Are rescue personnel trained in first aid and CPR and immediately available?

☐ Is there an effective communication system in place whenever respiratory equipment is used and the employee in the confined space is out of sight of the attendant?

☐ Is approved respiratory equipment required if the atmosphere inside the confined space cannot be made acceptable?

☐ Is all portable electrical equipment used inside confined spaces either grounded and insulated or equipped with ground-fault protection?

☐ Before gas welding or burning is started in a confined space, are hoses checked for leaks, compressed gas bottles forbidden inside the confined space, torches lighted only outside the confined space area, and the confined space area tested for an explosive atmosphere each time before a lighted torch is taken into the confined space?

☐ When using oxygen-consuming equipment (such as sala-manders, torches, or furnaces) in a confined space, is air provided to ensure combustion without reducing the oxygen concentration of the atmosphere below 19.5 percent by volume?

☐ Whenever combustion-type equipment is used in a confined space, are provisions made to ensure that the exhaust gases are vented outside the enclosure?

☐ Is each confined space checked for decaying vegetation or animal matter, which may produce methane?

☐ Is the confined space checked for possible industrial waste that could contain toxic properties?

☐ If the confined space is below the ground and near areas where motor vehicles are operating, is it possible for vehicle exhaust or carbon monoxide to enter the space?

Environmental Controls

☐ Are all work areas properly lighted?

☐ Are hazardous substances identified that may cause harm by inhalation, ingestion, skin absorption, or contact?

☐ Are employees aware of the hazards involved with the various chemicals they may be exposed to in their work environment, such as ammonia, chlorine, epoxies, and caustics?

☐ Is employee exposure to chemicals in the workplace kept within acceptable levels? Can a less harmful method or product be used?

☐ Is the work area's ventilation system appropriate for the work being performed?

☐ Are proper precautions being taken when handling asbestos and other fibrous materials?

☐ Are caution labels and signs used to warn of asbestos?

☐ Is the possible presence of asbestos determined prior to the beginning of any repair, demolition, construction, or reconstruction work?

☐ Are asbestos-covered surfaces kept in good repair to prevent release of fibers?

☐ Are wet methods used (when practicable) to prevent emission or airborne asbestos fibers, silica dust, and similar hazardous materials?

☐ Is vacuuming with appropriate equipment conducted, rather than blowing or sweeping dust?

☐ Are grinders, saws, and other machines that produce respirable dusts vented to an industrial collector or central exhaust system?

☐ Are all local exhaust ventilation systems designed and operated properly (at the airflow and volume necessary) for the application? Are the ducts free of obstructions? Have you checked to ensure that the belts are not slipping?

☐ Is personal protective equipment provided, used, and maintained whenever required?

☐ Are there written standard operating procedures for the selection and use of respirators?

☐ Are rest rooms and washrooms kept clean and sanitary?

☐ Is all water provided for drinking, washing, and cooking potable?

☐ Are all outlets for water that is not suitable for drinking clearly identified?

☐ Are employees instructed in the proper manner of lifting heavy objects?

☐ Where heat is a problem, have all fixed work areas been provided with a proper means of cooling?

☐ Are employees working on streets and roadways, where they are exposed to the hazards of traffic, required to wear high-visibility clothing?

☐ Are exhaust stacks and air intakes located so that contaminated air will not be recirculated within a building or other enclosed area?

Flammable and Combustible Materials

☐ Are combustible scrap, debris, and waste materials stored in covered metal receptacles and removed from the work site promptly?

☐ Are proper storage methods used to minimize the risk of fire and spontaneous combustion?

☐ Are approved containers and tanks used for the storage and handling of flammable and combustible liquids?

☐ Are all connections on drums and combustible liquid piping (vapor and liquid) tight?

☐ Are all flammable liquids kept in closed containers when not in use?

☐ Are bulk drums of flammable liquids grounded and bonded to containers during dispensing?

☐ Do storage rooms for flammable and combustible liquids have explosion-proof lights?

☐ Do storage rooms for flammables and combustible liquids have mechanical or gravity ventilation?

☐ Are safe practices followed when liquid petroleum gas is stored, handled, and used?

☐ Are liquefied petroleum storage tanks guarded to prevent damage from vehicles?

☐ Are all solvent wastes and flammable liquids kept in fire-resistant, covered containers until they are removed from the work site?

☐ Is vacuuming used whenever possible, rather than blowing or sweeping combustible dust?

☐ Are fire separators placed between containers of combustibles or flammables when stacked one upon another (to ensure their support and stability)?

☐ Are fuel gas cylinders and oxygen cylinders separated by distance, fire-resistant barriers, or other means while in storage?

☐ Are fire extinguishers provided for the type of materials they will extinguish and placed in areas where they are to be used (Class A: ordinary combustible materials fires; Class B: flammable liquid, gas, or grease fires; Class C: energized electrical equipment fires)?

☐ If a halon 1301 fire extinguisher is used, can employees evacuate within the specified time (for that extinguisher)?

☐ Are appropriate fire extinguishers mounted within 75 feet of outside areas containing flammable liquids and within 10 feet of any inside storage area for such materials?

☐ Is the transfer or withdrawal of flammable or combustible liquids performed by trained personnel?

☐ Are fire extinguishers mounted so that employees do not

have to travel more than 75 feet for a Class A fire or 50 feet for a Class B fire?

☐ Are employees trained in the use of fire extinguishers?

☐ Are all extinguishers serviced, maintained, and tagged at intervals not to exceed one year? Is a record maintained of required monthly checks of extinguishers?

Electrical Safety

☐ Are your workplace electricians familiar with OSHA electrical safety rules?

☐ Do you require compliance with OSHA rules on all contract electrical work?

☐ Are all employees required to report as soon as practical any obvious hazard to life or property observed in connection with electrical equipment or lines?

☐ Are employees instructed to make preliminary inspections and/or appropriate tests to determine what conditions exist before starting work on electrical equipment or lines?

☐ When electrical equipment or lines are to be serviced, maintained, or adjusted, are necessary switches opened, locked out, and tagged?

☐ Are portable handheld electrical tools and equipment grounded, or are they of the double-insulated type?

☐ Are electrical appliances such as vacuum cleaners, polishers, and vending machines grounded?

☐ Do extension cords have a grounding conductor? Are multiple plug adapters prohibited?

☐ Are ground-fault circuit interrupters installed on each temporary 15- or 20-ampere, 120-volt AC circuit at locations where construction, demolition, modifications, alterations, or excavations are being performed?

☐ Are all temporary circuits protected by suitable disconnecting switches or plug connectors at the junction with permanent wiring?

☐ Is exposed wiring and cords with frayed or deteriorated insulation repaired or replaced promptly?

☐ Are flexible cords and cables free of splices or taps?

☐ Are clamps or other securing means provided on flexible

cords or cables at plugs, receptacles, tools, and equipment, and is the cord jacket securely held in place?

☐ Are all cords, cable, and raceway connections intact and secure?

☐ In wet or damp locations, are electrical tools and equipment appropriate for the use of locations (or otherwise protected)?

☐ Is the location of electrical power lines and cables (overhead, underground, underfloor, other side of walls) determined before digging, drilling, or similar work is started?

☐ Is the use of metal measuring tapes, ropes, hand lines, or similar devices with metallic thread woven into the fabric prohibited where these could come into contact with energized parts of equipment or circuit conductors?

☐ Is the use of metal ladders prohibited in areas where the ladder or the person using the ladder could come into contact with energized parts of equipment, fixtures, or circuit conductors?

☐ Are all disconnecting switches and circuit breakers labeled to indicate their use or equipment served?

☐ Are disconnecting means always opened before fuses are replaced?

☐ Do all interior wiring systems include provisions for grounding metal parts or electrical raceways, equipment, and enclosures?

☐ Are all electrical raceways and enclosures securely fastened in place?

☐ Are all energized parts of electrical circuits and equipment guarded against accidental contact by approved cabinets or enclosures?

☐ Is sufficient access and working space provided and maintained around all electrical equipment to permit ready and safe operations and maintenance?

☐ Are all unused openings (including conduit knockouts) of electrical enclosures and fittings closed with appropriate covers, plugs, or plates?

☐ Are electrical enclosures such as switches, receptacles, and junction boxes provided with tightly fitting covers or plates?

☐ Are employees prohibited from working alone on energized lines or equipment over 600 volts?

☐ Are employees forbidden from working closer than 10 feet of high-voltage (over 750 volts) lines?

Noise

☐ Are there areas in your workplace where continuous noise levels exceed 85 decibels (dBA)?

☐ Are noise levels being measured using a sound level meter or an octave band analyzer, and records of these levels being kept?

☐ Have you tried isolating noisy machinery from the rest of your operation? Have engineering controls been used to reduce excessive noise?

☐ Where engineering controls are not feasible, are administrative controls (worker rotation) being used to minimize individual employee exposure to noise?

☐ Is there an ongoing preventive health program to educate employees in safe levels of noise and exposure, effects of noise on their health, and use of personal protection?

☐ Are employees who are exposed to continuous noise above 85 dBA retrained annually?

☐ Have work areas where noise levels make voice communication difficult been identified and posted?

☐ Is approved hearing protection equipment (noise-attenuating devices) used by every employee working in areas where noise levels exceed 90 dBA?

☐ Are employees properly fitted and instructed in the proper use and care of hearing protection?

☐ Are employees exposed to continuous noise above 85 dBA given periodic audiometric testing to ensure that you have an effective hearing protection system?

Identification of Piping Systems

☐ When nonpotable water is piped through a facility, are outlets or tabs posted to alert employees that it is unsafe and not to be used for drinking, washing, or personal use?

☐ When hazardous substances are transported through aboveground piping, is each pipeline identified?

☐ Have asbestos-covered pipelines been identified?

☐ When pipelines are identified by color-painted bands or tapes, are these located at reasonable intervals and at each outlet, valve, or connection?

☐ When pipelines are identified by color, is the color code posted at all locations where confusion could introduce hazards to employees?

☐ When the contents of pipelines are identified by name or abbreviations, is the information readily visible on the pipe near each valve or outlet?

☐ When pipelines carrying hazardous substances are identified by tags, are the tags constructed of durable material, the message clearly and permanently distinguishable, and tags installed at each valve or outlet?

☐ When pipelines are heated by electricity, steam, or another external source, are suitable warning signs or tags placed at unions, valves, or other serviceable parts of the system?

Materials Handling

☐ Are materials stored in a manner to prevent sprain or strain injuries to employees when retrieving the materials?

☐ Is there safe clearance for equipment through aisles and doorways?

☐ Are aisles permanently marked and kept clear to allow safe passage?

☐ Are motorized vehicles and mechanized equipment inspected daily or prior to use?

☐ Are vehicles shut off and brakes set prior to loading and unloading?

☐ Are containers of combustibles or flammables, when stacked while being moved, always separated by dunnage sufficient to provide stability?

☐ Are dock boards (bridge plates) used when loading and unloading operations are taking place between vehicles and docks?

☐ Are trucks and trailers secured from movement during loading and unloading?

☐ Are dock plates and loading ramps constructed and maintained with sufficient strength to support imposed loading?

☐ Are hand trucks maintained in safe operating condition?

☐ Are chutes equipped with side boards of sufficient height to prevent materials from falling off?

☐ Are chutes and gravity roller sections firmly placed or secured to prevent displacement?

☐ At the delivery end of rollers or chutes, are provisions made to brake the movement of materials?

☐ Are materials handled at a uniform level to prevent lifting or twisting injuries?

☐ Are material-handling aids used to lift or transfer heavy or awkward objects?

☐ Are pallets usually inspected before loading and moving?

☐ Are hooks with safety latches or other devices used when hoisting materials so that slings or load attachments won't accidentally slip off the hoist hooks?

☐ Are securing chains, ropes, chokes, or slings adequate for the job being performed?

☐ When hoisting materials or equipment, are provisions made to ensure that no one will be passing under suspended loads?

Transporting Employees and Materials

☐ Do employees operating vehicles on public thoroughfares have operator licenses?

☐ Are motor vehicle drivers trained in defensive driving and proper use of the vehicle?

☐ Are seat belts provided, and are employees required to use them?

☐ Does each van, bus, or truck routinely used to transport employees have an adequate number of seats?

☐ When employees are transported by truck, are provisions provided to prevent their falling from the vehicle?

☐ When transporting employees, are vehicles equipped with

lamps, brakes, horns, mirrors, windshields, and turn signals that are in good repair?

☐ Are transport vehicles provided with handrails, steps, stirrups, or similar devices that have been placed and arranged so employees can safely mount or dismount?

☐ Is a fully charged fire extinguisher in good condition with at least 4 B:C rating maintained in each employee transport vehicle?

☐ When cutting tools with sharp edges are carried in passenger compartments of employee transport vehicles, are they placed in closed boxes or containers that are secured in place?

☐ Are employees prohibited from riding on top of any load that can shift, topple, or otherwise become unstable?

☐ Are materials that could shift and enter the cab secured or barricaded?

Split Rim and Multipiece Wheel Tire Inflation

☐ Where tires are mounted and/or inflated on drop center wheels, is a safe-practice procedure posted and enforced?

☐ Where tires are mounted and/or inflated on wheels with split rims and/or retainer rings, is a safe-practice procedure posted and enforced?

☐ Does each tire inflation hose have a clip-on chuck with at least 24 inches of hose between the chuck and an inline valve and gauge?

☐ Does the tire inflation control valve automatically shut off the airflow when the valve is released?

☐ Is a tire-restraining device such as a cage rack used while inflating tires mounted on split rims or rims using retainer rings?

☐ Are employees strictly forbidden from taking a position directly over or in front of a tire while it is being inflated?

Cranes and Hoists

☐ Are cranes visually inspected for defective components prior to the start of any work shift?

☐ Are all electrically operated cranes effectively grounded?

☐ Is a crane preventive maintenance program established?
☐ Is the load chart clearly visible to the operator?
☐ Are all operators trained and provided with the operator's manual for the particular crane being operated?
☐ Have construction industry crane operators been issued a valid operator's card?
☐ Are operating controls clearly identified?
☐ Is a fire extinguisher provided at the operator's station?
☐ Is the rated capacity visibly marked on each crane?
☐ Is an audible warning device mounted on each crane?
☐ Is sufficient lighting provided for the operator to perform the work safely?
☐ Are cranes with booms that could fall over backward equipped with boom stops?
☐ Does each crane have a certificate indicating that required testing and examinations have been performed?
☐ Are crane inspection and maintenance records maintained and available for inspection?

Emergency Action Plan

☐ Have you developed an emergency action plan?
☐ Have emergency escape procedures and routes been developed and communicated to all employees?
☐ Do employees who must remain to operate critical plant operations before evacuating know the proper procedures?
☐ Is the employee alarm system that provides warning for emergency action recognizable and perceptible above ambient conditions?
☐ Are alarm systems properly maintained and tested regularly?
☐ Is the emergency action plan reviewed and revised periodically?
☐ Do employees know their responsibilities for reporting emergencies? During an emergency? For performing rescue and medical duties?

Infection Control

☐ Are employees potentially exposed to infectious agents in body fluids?

☐ Have occasions of potential occupational exposure been identified and documented?

☐ Have training and information programs been provided for employees exposed to or potentially exposed to blood and regulated body fluids?

☐ Have infection control procedures been instituted where appropriate, such as ventilation, universal precautions, workplace practices, and personal protective equipment?

☐ Are employees aware of specific workplace practices to follow when appropriate (hand washing, handling sharp instruments, handling of laundry, disposal of contaminated materials, reusable equipment, etc.)?

☐ Is personal protective equipment provided to employees and in all appropriate locations?

☐ Is the necessary equipment (mouthpieces, resuscitation bags, other ventilation devices) provided for administering mouth-to-mouth resuscitation on potentially infected patients?

☐ Are facilities/equipment to comply with workplace practices available, such as hand-washing sinks, biohazard tags and labels, containers for sharp objects, and detergents/disinfectants to clean up spills?

☐ Are all equipment and environmental and working surfaces cleaned and disinfected after contact with blood or potentially infectious materials?

☐ Is infectious waste placed in closable, leakproof containers, bags, or puncture-resistant holders with proper labels?

☐ Has medical surveillance, including HBV evaluation, antibody testing, and vaccination, been made available to potentially exposed employees?

☐ How often is training done? Does it cover universal precautions? Personal protective equipment? Workplace practices that should include blood drawing, room cleaning, laundry handling, and cleanup of blood spills? Needlestick exposure/management? Hepatitis B vaccination?

Ergonomics

☐ Can the work be performed without eyestrain or glare to the employees?

☐ Can the task be done without the worker's having to hold his/her elbows out and away from the body?

☐ Can workers keep their hands/wrists in a neutral position when working?

☐ Are mechanical assists available to the worker performing materials-handling tasks?

☐ Can the task be done without having to stoop the neck and shoulder to view the work?

☐ Are pressure points on any part of the body (wrists, forearms, back of thighs) being avoided?

☐ Can the work be done using the larger muscles of the body?

☐ Are there sufficient rest breaks, in addition to the regular rest breaks, to relieve stress from repetitive motion tasks?

☐ Are tools, instruments, and machinery shaped, positioned, and handled so that tasks can be performed comfortably?

☐ Are all pieces of furniture adjusted, positioned, and arranged to minimize strain on the body?

☐ Are unnecessary distances eliminated when moving materials?

☐ Are lifts confined within the knuckle-to-shoulder zone?

☐ Does the task require fixed work postures?

☐ Is work arranged so that workers are not required to lift and carry too much weight?

☐ If workers have to push or pull objects using great amounts of force, are mechanical aids provided?

Ventilation for Indoor Air Quality

☐ Does your HVAC system provide at least the quantity of outdoor air designed into the system at the time the building was constructed?

☐ Is the HVAC system inspected at least annually and maintained in a clean and efficient manner?

☐ Are efforts made to purchase furnishings or building treatments that do not give off toxic or offensive vapors?

☐ Are indoor air quality complaints investigated and the results conveyed to workers?

Video Display Terminals (VDTs)

☐ Can the work be performed without eyestrain or glare to the employees?

- [ ] Can workers keep their hands/wrists in a neutral position when working?
- [ ] Can the task be done without having to stoop the neck and shoulders to view the task?
- [ ] Are pressure points on any part of the body (wrists, forearms, back of thighs) being avoided?
- [ ] Are there sufficient rest breaks, in addition to the regular rest breaks, to relieve stress from repetitive motion tasks?
- [ ] Are all pieces of furniture adjusted, positioned, and arranged to minimize strain on the body?
- [ ] Are fixed work postures avoided in the task?
- [ ] Do the VDT workstations meet the recommended criteria:
- [ ] Height of work surface: adjustable 23 to 28 inches.
- [ ] Width of work surface: 30 inches.
- [ ] Viewing distance: 16 to 22 inches for close-range focusing.
- [ ] Thickness of work surface: 1 inch.
- [ ] Eyes in relation to screen: topmost line of display should be at approximately eye level (or lower for bifocal wearers).
- [ ] Knee room height: minimum of 26.2 inches nonadjustable surface and 24 inches adjustable surface.
- [ ] Knee room width: 20 inches.
- [ ] Knee room depth: minimum of 15 inches knee level, 23.5 inches toe level.
- [ ] Seat height: adjustable 16 to 20.5 inches.
- [ ] Seat size: 13 to 17 inches depth, 17.1 inches to 20 inches width, "waterfall" front edge.
- [ ] Seat slope: adjustable 0 degrees to 10 degrees backward slope.
- [ ] Backrest size: 15 to 20 inches high, 13 inches wide.
- [ ] Backrest height: adjustable 3 to 6 inches above seat.
- [ ] Backrest tilt: adjustable 15 degrees.
- [ ] Angle between backrest and seat: 90 degrees to 105 degrees.
- [ ] Angle between seat and lower leg: 60 degrees to 100 degrees.
- [ ] Angle between upper arm and forearm in relation to keyboard: upper arm and forearm should form a right angle (90 degrees); hands should be in a reasonably straight line with the forearm.

☐ Nonadjustable work surfaces: table surface should be about 29 inches with a keyboard surface height of 27 inches

☐ VDT stands: height-adjustable stands for all new installations.

☐ Seats: easily adjustable swivel chairs on five-point base.

☐ Footrests: If operator cannot keep both feet flat on floor when chair height is properly adjusted to work surface.

☐ Keyboards: thin, detached from console, palm rest.

☐ Nonkeyboard-entry devices: position devices following same guidelines for keyboards.

☐ Screens: readable with no perceptible flicker, brightness control necessary.

☐ Blink rate: no more than two different blink rates, at least 2 hertz (Hz) apart—slow blink rate not less than 0.8 Hz, fast blink rate not more than 5 Hz.

☐ Do the VDT workstations meet the recommended criteria for glare control?

☐ VDT screen placed at right angles to windows; screens have tilt and swivel adjustments.

☐ Windows with curtains, drapes, or blinds to reduce bright outside light.

☐ Lighting levels at 30–50 foot-candles when using a VDT; 50–70 foot-candles where documents are read, compared to normal office levels of 75–160 foot-candles.

☐ Diffusers, cube louvers, or parabolic louvers to reduce overhead lighting glare.

☐ Work surfaces with antiglare (matte) finish.

☐ Movable task or desk lights; VDTs located between rows of overhead lighting; screen filters and/or hoods if above is not successful.

☐ Are cables and cords concealed, covered, or otherwise safely out of the way?

☐ Is additional ventilation or air-conditioning sufficient to overcome heat generated by more than one VDT workstation in the same room?

☐ Are temperature and humidity controlled to maintain thermal comfort and 30–60 percent relative humidity?

☐ Are there acoustical enclosures for printers if sound levels exceed 55 dBA? Are main CPUs and disk drives isolated?

☐ Are operators taught how to adjust chairs, workstation heights, screen brightness, and instructed in correct seat posture?

☐ Is there fatigue control through good operator posture, body and eye exercises, rest pauses, job rotation, or substitution of less demanding tasks?

☐ Are operators evaluated for visual problems?

☐ Are there operator involvement in selection process, communication between operators and supervisors, user-friendly software, and adequate operator training?

Index